FCK THE BAR

TAKE YOUR PLACE AT COUNSEL TABLE

JESSICA KLEIN

FCK THE BAR: Take Your Place at Counsel Table

Second Edition.

ISBN: 9781096594628

For further information, please visit: www.FckTheBar.com or www.FTBBarPrep.com.

Photo: Sarah Lin Photography

CONTENTS

1

FUCK THE BAR

Fuck the bar exam. No, really. Fuck it. This exam cannot stop you from taking your place at counsel table. It's just a test. Did you hear what I said? *Really hear it?*

It. is. just. a. test.

If there's anything you know how to do my friend, it's take a test.

If you're sitting for the bar exam, I already know you have what it takes to pass. I know it because if you have already been successful as a law student, then you possess all the qualities necessary to pass the bar exam. You've already taken law school exams. You have a four-year degree (perhaps more). You took the LSAT, SAT, PSAT, graduated from high school, middle school, elementary school, and likely even preschool. You have been a student for twenty years. T w e n t y y e a r s . Two entire decades. It's insane, really.

Without a doubt, you know how to be a successful test taker. You've spent years going to classes, reading, and studying, so you have the ambition to achieve. All those years you've worked, just for the mere opportunity to sit for the bar exam, demonstrate your discipline and industriousness. You are ambitious. Smart. Driven. Capable. Disciplined. You have taken innumerable tests. Despite all that, it's probable you've suddenly developed serious angst over this particular test if you're like most other bar takers. If you don't know it already, let me tell you: you have what it takes to pass one more test. That is all the bar exam is: a test.

So yeah. Fuck the bar. If anybody's got this, you do. You've been training for this shit the last twenty years. The bar exam is not going to stop you from taking your seat at counsel table. If I've articulated my message successfully, then by the time you finish reading this book, your feelings around the bar exam will be:

> *I've worked way too long and way too hard to let this motherfucker stand in the way of me getting on with my badass life. Fuck that. Where's my chair? I'm going to sit here at counsel table and get comfortable. In fact, I'll take that big cushy chair over there, thankyouverymuch.*

You will be bearing down on the bar exam full throttle in anticipatory excitement as a runner sprints in the last stretch of their race.

Although this mindset is the goal, you're probably not feeling entirely on board just yet. But why not? If the bar exam is only a test, then why freak out? It's because bar exam lore has gotten out of hand and it feeds a reputation that isn't of service to you or other bar takers. The bar exam needs to be knocked down to size. It's gotten waaaaaaay too big for its britches over the years.

This monstrous reputation is built as you advance in education. The further along you get in academia, the fewer exams you take. As the number of exams shrinks, their importance has more bearing on your future success. All of which add up to bigger stakes. Bigger stakes = more stress. More stress = diminished test performance.

It certainly doesn't help that all of a sudden the academic rules changed in law school. In law school, you're only smart *as compared to* your classmates. You also get no feedback on your grasp of the concepts until the course is entirely over and you show up for your single exam. Add to that pressure the fact that you might not get the job you want if you don't get a high enough mark on every single exam, which is a problem when you have mortgaged your future with astronomical debt. So after having your confidence challenged the last three years, and when the stakes are highest, you must take the longest and hardest exam of your life.

No wonder so many students get fucked up in the head over the bar exam. You, like so many other bar takers, are ambitious, smart, driven, capable, and disciplined. Yet you've likely bought into the idea that somehow this exam is so incredibly different. Or perhaps that you are for some reason inept at studying for and passing it unless you pay thousands of dollars to specialized companies to teach you how to study for the test. As if you've never taken a fucking test before.

People! Let me remind you who the fuck you are. You are the shit! You have a brilliant mind. You are ambitious. You are industrious. You are a veteran test taker. You are incredibly capable, and the bar exam isn't going to change any of those facts.

You have been learning for the last twenty years how to consume information, roll it around inside your brain long enough to understand it, and then regurgitate it in whatever format your teacher wants you to. If they said: write a book report, you wrote a book report. If they said: write a poem, you wrote a poem. If they said: show the math, you showed the math. If they said: write a ten-page report with an introduction, five main points, and a conclusion, then you wrote a ten-page report with an introduction, five main points, and a conclusion.

So guess what you need to do on the bar exam? The same damn thing you've been doing the past twenty years - giving the teacher precisely what he or she wants in the format he or she wants it. It really is that easy. The bar exam is just one more time that you do exactly what you've done a hundred times before. You knew what to do on all those other tests. You took the information that the instructor gave you during the course, and you demonstrated your knowledge and understanding in whatever format he or she asked you to. That's all you did on those tests. And that's all you have to do on this test. Because the bar exam is a test. It. is. just. a. test.

Yes, the content is more sophisticated. But that's not a problem because if the content was too difficult for you, you wouldn't have gotten into and graduated law school. The content isn't the issue.

The issue is that you believe the bar exam is unlike any test you've ever taken before and that none of your past twenty years of education is any good on this test. Although it's true that the bar exam *is* unlike any test you have taken before, you *can still lean on* your decades of education to carry you through. This book will show you HOW to take your already existing test-taking capabilities and prepare for this test. The pages of this book contain a workable and proven strategy that applies to all U.S. bar exams (with variances in materials for each jurisdiction).

This book will show you how to walk into exam day with a skip in your step because 1) you are finally checking off that last to-do from your "Things I Have To Do To Get On With My Life" list, and, 2) you know you're going to own that bar exam like the boss you are. I simplify the bar exam by breaking it down into its simple component parts and layout a completely do-able strategy to get you ready to walk into the bar exam with every confidence in the world.

Painless Bar Prep

If you were shocked when you first saw the title Fck The Bar - good! The name is intentionally irreverent, unorthodox, and unapologetic. I hope to challenge preconceptions and shock people into thinking about the bar differently.

But guess what? That's not the only shocker in this book. Here's the next one: I firmly believe the bar exam can be painless.

There's a common bar exam perception that this test is some mythical beast which requires struggle and mental anguish to slay. In an effort to overcome this challenge, people typically throw out all semblance of a balanced lifestyle. They will study *sixteen hours a day*.

The bar exam does not leave their consciousness. Not even when they sleep. Anxiety and nightmares plague them even there.

This is bullshit. The bar exam is a test. You are hereby granted permission to go through the bar prep process feeling calm, confident, prepared, organized, rested, supported, and even - *gasp!* - enjoying your life during the process. You can change the way you view (and subsequently experience) the bar exam.

I 100% believe that it is possible to prepare for and pass the bar exam with confidence and a positive outlook! I know it's possible because I've done it, and I've helped others do it, too. In this book I show you how to do it, step by step.

The reason people are stressed out, anxious, and lose all sense of balance during bar prep is because they feel overwhelmed (out of control because they don't truly understand what the bar exam encompasses) and do not have confidence in their study approach. Also, they waste time on ineffective tasks that don't translate into true progress. They know this! Deep down they realize their busyness is *not* getting them ready to pass the exam so they are worried constantly.

Having an effective and powerful plan for success, and *executing* that plan day in and day out eliminates the anxiety and stress, and allows you to remain a whole, well-balanced person throughout.

2

FIGHT CLUB

I f you've gone to law school, you already know that the magical thing that happens in law school is that your brain becomes unalterably changed: you learn to think differently. You learn to think like a lawyer.

You also know two hard truths about what law school does not do for you: (1) it does not teach you how to practice law, and (2) it does not prepare you for the bar exam. No one is ready to sit for the bar exam the day after graduation.

So let me ask you a question: if you are not ready to take the bar exam the day after graduation - after you've studied the law for three years under the instruction of brilliant professors who are subject matter experts - then why would a few more months of doing that same thing make you ready for the bar?

I don't think it does.

———

Preparing for and passing the bar exam is a much, much simpler proposition than everyone thinks it is. Traditional bar prep, which involves hours and hours of lectures, book after book of outlines, and all sorts of other study activities *other than* practicing the MBE, essays and performance tests, is completely unnecessary.

My suspicion is that bar prep activities such as watching lectures and reading outlines developed as a solution to what bar examinees *wanted*, not what they *needed*.

If I had to hazard a guess, I would guess that if I sat you down to take a practice bar exam *today*, you would protest and explain that you can't take a practice test because you don't know enough yet. You don't think you know the subject matter; you're "not ready." So it makes sense that bar prep companies created programs to solve the problem you *think* you have of "not knowing enough" so you could *feel* prepared to take the bar exam. I stress the word *feel* because you can *feel* ready by knowing every single little bit of black letter law like the back of your hand and still not actually *be* ready to *perform* well on the bar exam.

If you've seen the movie *Fight Club*, you will be able to recite the first and second rules of Fight Club at the drop of a hat.

> The first rule of Fight Club is: You do not talk about Fight Club.
> The second rule of Fight Club is: You do not talk about Fight Club.

Likewise, anyone who reads this book should be able to immediately recite the first and second rules of the bar exam.

> The first rule of the bar exam is: Nothing matters except performance.
> The second rule of the bar exam is: Nothing matters except performance.

Nothing matters except performance! If you are doing anything that doesn't improve your bar exam <u>performance</u>, you are wasting your time.

If you don't perform well on the exam you won't get enough points, the bar graders will fail you, and you don't get to sit at counsel table. So everything revolves around performance. It's not until you fully understand how pivotal performance is that you can properly view your study efforts. When you have bar exam performance as your goal, you can reverse engineer everything else and understand the actions you need to take.

Legal knowledge is NOT the goal. It is necessary, but not sufficient. Performing well enough on the bar exam that you get your name on the pass list is the goal. Performance is very, very, VERY different than knowledge. Incredibly different. Sit with that for a moment and let it sink in. Think about all the ways in which you already know that to be true. From things as rudimentary as learning to walk or tying your shoe - these are things which you "knew how to do" the moment you could perform them.

If you are like most people who learned how to drive a car around the age of sixteen, you first started your learning process by watching other drivers drive while you were a passenger in the car, reading the driver test booklet, being told what all the pedals, levers, and buttons did, and learning what the traffic signs and rules of the road were. However, none of that knowledge made you a driver. How could it? None of those things even got you into the driver's seat. No, it wasn't until you got behind the wheel of the car, started the car, and began to perform the act of driving that you crossed the threshold to becoming a driver. Performance is different from knowledge.

When you finally started performing the act of driving, I bet you weren't so great at it. It's a skill. You have to log hours actually driving - aka practicing - to become more comfortable with the car, with the roads, with the traffic signs, with other drivers, with increased speed, in new conditions, in the rain, etc. You get better and better because you were practicing, not because you spent additional hours reading the driver booklet.

Think about how many times you had to practice parallel parking before you could successfully *do* it. If you still can't really do it right, or if you drive around the block to find an alternate parking spot because you hate to parallel park, you're not alone. Plenty of people still dread it. It takes a lot of practice to become skilled at that. That's because "knowing" the steps to properly parallel park, such as how to line up your mirrors, turn the wheel, straighten out at the proper moment, and all the other parts that go into it mean *absolutely nothing* when it comes to *doing it*. That's because *nothing matters except performance.*

In so many areas of life, knowledge is meaningless, and performance is everything. Think of learning to play an instrument, learning a new language, learning to paint, learning to cook, or learning a sport. To learn any of these things requires a basic understanding of the concepts (i.e., knowledge), but that isn't what is meant when someone says, for example, "I know how to speak French." Knowledge is necessary, but not sufficient. Knowing how to conjugate a verb in a foreign language is a necessary part of learning that language, but no one would say you know that language until you can speak (i.e., perform) that language. Again, *nothing matters except performance.*

Our lives are filled with performances - skills we can DO without thought because at one point in our lives, we performed the act for the first time. We tried something. Then tried again, and again. It required action. For each one of these daily skills that we can now do without much difficulty, we learned because we did. And we became proficient because we took repeated action.

Passing the bar exam is truly the same thing. When you understand and believe this concept, you won't look at bar prep the same way again. You will have no interest in cracking open an outline again. You won't write out flashcards. You won't listen to a single lecture. Why? Because by and large they're a complete waste of your precious time since you will perform none of those things on the actual bar exam. Remember the first rule of the bar exam is: *Nothing matters except performance.*

At no point during the actual bar exam will you be asked to give a lecture, read an outline, or write out a stack of flashcards. No bar grader is going to give you points for how many mnemonics you memorized. Therefore, practicing those tasks does nothing for improving your bar exam performance. They are learning tasks, not performance tasks. You just spent three years learning. You've already checked that box and got it covered, so now it's over and done with. The knowledge is already inside your head. You don't need more of that to pass the bar exam. Really!

This is why everyone says that going to law school does not prepare you for the bar exam. This is what they're talking about. The knowledge you have gained is vital for learning to think like a lawyer, learning core legal principles, and being able to practice law. That knowledge is necessary, but not sufficient, for passing the bar exam. Those who pass the bar exam are those who can successfully perform the bar exam tasks.

Time spent doing what has collectively become known as "bar prep" (writing outlines, reading outlines, listening to lectures, doing worksheets, creating flashcards, reading flashcards, memorizing mnemonics and rule statements, studying attack sheets, etc.) is not only a waste of your time because it only moves the needle incrementally, if at all, but it can be dangerous. The danger comes from the false sense of security you gain when you've spent day after day doing these things, thinking that you are more ready to write a passing essay answer now than you were before you did those things.

Additionally, if you spend twelve hours one day reviewing flashcards, watching lectures, and memorizing mnemonics, you'll likely feel like you've made a significant amount of progress. You may begin to erroneously equate busyness with effectiveness. The tasks that are keeping you busy are only as effective as the result they have on your bottom line. If you cannot write a better essay at the end of the day than at the beginning of the day, you have wasted your time.

Even if you "know more" after spending those twelve hours, it does not mean you are going to be able to write a passing essay if you have problems with your writing, analysis, organization, issue spotting, or some other aspect of essay performance. Your ability to regurgitate an accurate rule statement is necessary but not sufficient to get a passing score. You can perfectly list every applicable rule statement in your essay answer and still fail if you don't have all the other aspects of successful essay writing on board. We'll get into what is necessary for a passing essay answer later on, but I want to make the point: *legal knowledge is different from successful bar exam performance.*

On multiple occasions I have heard from bar exam repeaters who had taken big name bar prep courses their first time around that they were overworked and therefore overconfident going into the bar exam, only to find out they were actually underprepared. *Busyness gave them a false sense of security,* and sadly, they paid the bitter price of trusting their knowledge instead of perfecting their performance.

Nothing Matters Except Performance

3

HACKING THE BAR EXAM

S ome alternative titles for this book could have been "Hacking the Bar Exam" or "The Bar Exam: Deconstructed." That's because if you look at the component parts which constitute the bar exam, you will see it's not a big, complicated, unwieldy beast after all. Let's unpack it.

1. The bar exam is a PREDICTABLE test.
2. Passing it comes down to the successful performance of very specific TASKS.
3. There are simple, calculated ACTIONS you can take to become proficient at those tasks.

PREDICTABLE

The bar exam is a predictable test. It isn't your typical law school exam where you hope and pray that you were able to discern throughout the semester what each professor intends to test on. The bar exam is not a game of "hide the ball." Luckily for you, there are years and years of previously administered bar exams available to you. For free. No one had to break into the principal's office to steal a copy of the test; the administrators of the bar exam actually go through the effort of publishing the past exams on their own websites FOR you.

When you take the time to go through the past exams - and believe me when I tell you you absolutely should if you want to pass - you will discover for yourself that there is an undeniable pattern. The bar examiners test the same material over and over. You do not need to know the entire breadth of the law to pass.

Like most areas in life, Pareto's principle (the 80/20 rule) applies here. Going through the past exams will show you that there are specific issues the examiners test over and over and over again. Moreover, there are some issues that the examiners rarely test.

If you're wise, you will make sure to focus your time and energy to learn the frequently-tested areas down cold. It is a waste of your precious time to treat all issues and rules equally. Some have a very slim likelihood of showing up on the exam while others have a very high probability of showing up on the exam. Therefore you do not want to spend your energy equally. It is better to spend your energy *proportionately*. This is where going through all the prior exams you can get your hands on will help. This is where things get predictable.

The only way for something to be predictable is by having prior experience with it. Let's look at a non-academic example. Everyone has that friend who runs late. When you first became friends with that person, you might have given them the benefit of the doubt the first couple of times, but after a while, you realized that they are just always late and it was part of their character. Once you realized that, you started to anticipate they were going to be late whenever you were going to meet up with them. And they didn't disappoint. They were late. But you knew they were going to be. They just always are.

The bar exam is predictable if you get to know it. For example, if you are taking the California Bar Exam, you can be sure that Professional Responsibility is going to be tested on the essay portion. If you're taking the Uniform Bar Exam, you can be sure that Civil Procedure is going to be tested on the essay portion. How do I know this? Because I've looked at the number of times they've been tested over the last ten years and with very rare exceptions, they are tested each and every time.

Get some experience with the bar exam under your belt. Use the prior exams. You will find out what to expect. If you open up an outline and start reading the law, you are going to be reading *everything* in Torts; *everything* in Contracts; *everything* in Evidence... you get the idea. But guess what? The bar exam *does not test everything*. Yes, you will be tested on Torts, Contracts, and Evidence. But only portions of them. So if you spend some time with the previous exams you will know which portions are going to show up. It's predictable.

Now on rare occasion your late friend shows up on time. Right? Sure they do. And sometimes the bar exam will throw in an outlier and test something that hasn't shown up before or only shows up very infrequently. If that happens, it's okay. I'll talk about this later on in the book and how to handle it. For now, know that if you have prepared for the bar exam in the manner outlined in this book, you are going to be so incredibly solid on so much of the exam that being surprised by a single issue isn't going to tank the entire thing.

The bar exam is predictable in an entirely other way, too. And here's where things get really, really good for you. Most jurisdictions publish examples of high scoring answers so you know what they're looking for! They are SHOWING YOU THE ANSWER KEY AHEAD OF TIME. No one is hiding the ball.

I think that since people are so used to these sample answers being available for free that they completely underestimate how incredibly valuable they are. It was Jim Rohn who said, "success leaves clues." And it is so true! In so many areas of life, there are people who have gone before, figured out a system that works, and become successful.

If your goal is to become a solo practitioner after you become licensed, you are probably interested in finding out how other solo practitioners whom you admire have structured their practice. You want to copy the successful ones, right? Or do you intend to flop around aimlessly and learn every lesson the hard way? Of course not.

Or let's say you intend to get into BigLaw and have a meteoric rise to the top. Your ambition and common sense tell you to take note of what your highly successful predecessors have done and then beat them at their own game. Am I right?

The bar exam is no different. There's a *clearly marked path* for you. You can see exactly what previous bar passers wrote on exams to achieve high scores. It's there for you to take advantage of. And more than that, the bar examiners want you to see it. They put it out there so this information will serve people. They're handing them out like high school nurses hand out condoms. They're saying: *Please, take some! Use these!*

For example, The State Bar of California publishes two selected answers for each essay and performance test right on their website to be accessed for free. The selected answers "were assigned high grades and were written by applicants who passed the examination after one read."

Having the sample answers is helpful for more than just the content of the answers. Sure, the answers contain the legal issues being tested, but they also show you how to draft a good answer. A good essay answer isn't just about knowing the law being tested, it's about regurgitating it in a particular format that the graders want to see. You need to present it in a certain fashion.

You wouldn't dump a pile of flour, sugar, salt, egg, vanilla, butter, baking soda, and baking powder on a plate and call it a cake. You have all the ingredients which are necessary to make a cake. But until you mix them together in the proper order and proportions, then bake it at the right temperature, and for the appropriate amount of time, you can't call it a cake.

The sample answers have what the bar graders are looking for. Your goal is to give the bar graders what they are looking for so they can award you as many points as possible. Later on, you'll learn how to take these examples and utilize them to your greatest benefit, and do so in a very simple way which makes the most effective and efficient use of your time.

4
TASKS

The second component part of hacking the bar exam comes down to the successful performance of very specific tasks. In most jurisdictions, the bar exam is broken down into these three tasks:

- The Multistate Bar Exam (MBE)
- State-specific essay questions or the Multistate Essay Exam (MEE)
- A state-specific performance test or the Multistate Performance Test (MPT)

Please note what is NOT on the exam:

- Reading outlines
- Creating outlines
- Reading flashcards
- Creating flashcards
- Writing mnemonics
- Listening to lectures

In short, there is no portion of the bar exam where you will be asked to provide a brain dump. No amount of legal knowledge inside your brain is going to get you a single point unless you can apply that knowledge in the proper format. I can't stress this enough. You can be incredibly smart and have tons of knowledge, but unless that knowledge gets transmitted to the bar graders, you get absolutely no points. As outlined above, there are only three formats in which you can demonstrate your knowledge: the MBE, essays, and performance tests.

These are the crucial tasks. If your bar prep activities are not *directly improving* your *performance* of these three tasks, then you are not studying as effectively as you can and should be. Activities which *indirectly* improve your bar exam performance are a poor use of your time, especially since they might not actually be improving your bar exam performance at all!

For example, if you fail the bar exam because you can't finish in time, it doesn't matter how many issues you can spot or how well you know the material! In this instance, activities such as memorizing flashcards or listening to lectures are doing you zero bit of good, and in fact, are eating up precious time that could be better spent by getting faster at the exam.

Here's another example. Let's say you know all the law and can spot all the issues, but you don't know how to apply the facts to the law and perform an analysis. If you have a bad habit of making conclusory statements, you are likely going to fail no matter how many outlines you read or how many mnemonics you know. Bar graders need to see that you know how to analyze facts. They couldn't give a shit how well you've got that mnemonic memorized.

Let's do one more example. For this example, we're going to use a performance test. Let's assume you've read the file and the library, and understand what type of task you're being asked to perform. You know what you want to say, but you just can't seem to get it from your brain and into your answer in a logical and methodical fashion. You get hung up on how to get it organized and presented in a lawyerly way.

When the reader looks at your answer, it's chaotic and disorganized and doesn't seem to demonstrate the information they're looking for. In a situation like this, it doesn't matter what is going on in your brain because the graders are not going to grade what you know. They are going to grade *the product*. That's all they have to go on.

At this point, it should be crystal clear that the only thing you're being scored on is your ability to perform these tasks. I've got some tough love for you: if you're not good at performing these tasks, you're not going to do well on the bar exam. It's as simple as that. But have no fear, there's an answer. In this book, I will teach you how you can get really good at performing those tasks.

———

The Gatekeepers

Before we move on and talk about the actions you can take to get good at performing these tasks, I want to pause and talk about an important group of people who are integral to you passing the bar exam: the bar graders.

Understanding why we have a bar exam in the first place, and how this plays out in your bar exam journey is helpful to framing your study approach.

With all this talk about "fuck the bar" and how to "hack" the bar exam, it may seem that I'm giving a big fat middle finger to the boards of bar examiners across the nation. Not at all true. Although this book has an irreverent and unapologetic title designed to shake things up a bit and hopefully get you to see the bar exam differently, I am not irreverent about the purpose the bar exam serves or about the legal profession itself. I wholeheartedly believe in the honor and dignity of the profession.

The legal profession is prestigious and should be filled with practitioners of utmost integrity. The things we do as lawyers are weighty and humbling. The public will trust us with life-altering responsibilities. As a lawyer, you will be fighting for the freedom of clients who face serious criminal charges and may lose their freedom to incarceration; you will be fighting to protect the multi-million dollar businesses of clients who have spent their lifetime building; you will be fighting for mothers and fathers who don't want to lose their children; you will be fighting for the ability of the indigent to keep a roof over their head and avoid homelessness.

The seriousness of this responsibility cannot be over emphasized. The consequences of allowing unfit persons to practice law is severe. Naturally, there must be standards and safeguards, which is why we have a bar exam in the first place.

The bar exam is a gatekeeper. It filters out the small percentage of individuals who have been accepted into and graduated law school but are unable to judiciously apply legal principles in a proficient enough manner to adequately represent the legal interests of the public. In this way, the bar exam provides an invaluable service not only to the legal profession but to the millions of individuals who seek legal services to carry them through some of the most challenging problems of their lives.

This is the *reason* we have a bar exam, and the bar graders are tasked with judging our competence through reading a single essay. Or a single performance test. Based on those few pages of written work that you submit, they will have to give you a score that reflects their judgment as to your fitness to practice law. Later, all the individual scores from the essays and performance tests are compiled with your MBE score, and ultimately you receive a passing or failing score.

Put yourself in the bar graders shoes... they need to do their best to decipher whether you have the minimum competence required to be able to go out into the world and handle these responsibilities. They only have a few pages of your written work to make that determination. You need to be able to prove to them through those pages that you are competent.

How do you do that? You write a damn good essay and performance test, as well as score well on the MBE. <u>These are the only three avenues by which you can prove your competence.</u> If you want a seat at the table - a seat at *counsel table* - you need to be able to keep up with everyone else sitting there. The bar exam is your chance to demonstrate that you can.

The bar graders are expecting and looking for a certain kind of work product. The people who pass the bar exam are the ones who take the raw black letter law and mix it together with the ability to spot legal issues and extract relevant facts, then combine those in an organized and logical way, fashion it all together with the proper language and tone, and polish it off with a reasoned legal conclusion, all while demonstrating sound judgment.

In essence, you are presenting the bar graders with a cake, not simply the pile of flour, sugar, salt, egg, vanilla, butter, baking soda, and baking powder that I referenced earlier. By taking these raw ingredients and putting them all together and presenting it to the bar graders in the correct way, they will be able to see through the lens of your essay answer that you know what *to do* with that raw knowledge: you know what's important, you know what the law is, you know how the law applies to that situation, you exercise good judgment, and you are intelligent enough.

If You're a Repeater

If you're a repeater, hear me out. Just because you have failed the bar exam one or more times, does NOT mean you should be filtered out from the practice of law. That is not what I'm saying here. The bar exam is designed to filter out people who do not have the competence to practice law. Chances are (and my experience tells me) you most likely failed for an entirely different reason. You may have had test anxiety, were unable to spend sufficient time preparing, did not take enough practice tests, or wasted time doing tasks that didn't help you perform on the exam.

There are many reasons you may have failed - reasons which are easily remedied once you identify them and take effective action. This will be made clear as you continue reading this book, and chapter 16 is devoted entirely to this. A few changes are most likely all that is needed to completely change your trajectory and get your name on the pass list.

5

ACTIONS

The last component part of hacking the bar exam comes down to taking the simple, calculated actions that will make you proficient at the bar exam tasks.

To become good at performing the bar exam tasks, there are specific actions you can take. It's just like getting good at driving. You're going to have to practice driving. Likewise, you should practice taking essays, performance tests, and MBEs. Over and over and over again. Do EXACTLY what you will be doing on the bar exam.

The old adage is so true: practice makes perfect. So for essays, you are going to sit down to take a timed practice essay, full length, using your complete concentration. Do not short cut this process by bullet-pointing your answers, issue spotting only, or skipping the conclusions. You will write it *as if you had to hand it into the bar graders.* You will do this for every essay subject, multiple times. The same goes for performance tests. The same goes for MBEs.

Curiously, almost everyone already understands and adopts this principle when it comes to the MBE. I've never met a bar examinee who needs to be convinced that they need to do practice MBEs in order to get ready for the bar exam. Nor do they think that they have to keep reading outlines because they don't know enough law to start doing MBEs. Instead, they usually jump right into practicing MBEs and do lots of them over the course of their bar prep - which is great! This is precisely the way all bar prep should be!

Where things go wrong is when bar examinees treat the essays and performance test portions of the exam differently. Just as it would be absurd to put off practicing MBEs until the very end of bar prep when they "know enough," it is dangerous to put off practicing essays and performance tests until the very end!

Struggling through an MBE question, getting it wrong, and then reading through the correct answer and its explanation is how you learn and improve your performance. It is the same process with the other portions of the exam. The earlier you start practicing essays and performance tests, the sooner you will learn and improve your performance.

Understandably, taking practice MBEs is more palatable than taking practice essays and performance tests. A practice MBE question literally takes less than two minutes, and all you have to do is select between four answer options that have already been provided to you.

A practice essay will take thirty to sixty minutes (depending on your jurisdiction), and you have to turn a blank document into a cogent written answer, drawing upon your legal knowledge and various other skills such as analytical thinking, judgment, organization, legal analysis, etc.

A performance test is going to take ninety minutes, and also requires you to rifle through pages and pages of raw material in the file and library before you even know what the answer should be.

It's a ton more work! If you're anything like me, the despicable thought of writing essays and performance tests day in and day out makes you want to groan.

I won't deny it - it's the advice no one wants to hear. No one wants to write essays. Reading outlines and flipping through flashcards is so much more preferable. Why? *Because it's easy.* Someone else had to do the hard work of getting that knowledge in their brain onto paper to create the outline or flashcard. You already know this to be true.

For example, reading this book is easy. Writing the book is a different story. Reading the book is fast. Writing it, not so much. Reading books does not make you a writer of books. Don't think that because you can consume the content, you can create the content. Going back to the driving analogy... don't think that because you've been a passenger in a car for sixteen years and know what it feels like to ride with a good driver that you can operate a vehicle in the same way. *Don't think that because you can read a well-written bar exam essay that you can create a well-written bar exam essay.* You must become good at it. And to become good at it, you must try - over and over again.

Reading outlines and model answers is also a passive activity. It doesn't challenge you. It doesn't show you where you are messing up or what you don't know. Writing essays, taking a performance, doing MBEs - this is stuff that no one can do for you. It sucks. It's hard (at first). It takes more effort and requires active engagement. But it's also what you have to do on the bar. Do the hard work now, and it will pay off big time.

If you do the work, you will find that you won't have to spend as many hours preparing as a lot of other examinees. Many people take commercial bar prep classes and spend most of their time listening to lectures, reading outlines, and creating outlines. They make checklists and flashcards. They re-read the outlines and checklists. They quiz themselves on the flashcards. These passive tasks become a massive portion of their preparation. Consider the simple fact that they are going to be in a class for hours each day, commute to and from class, take a lunch break, then commute to the library. Take note: they haven't even started studying yet! That's at least five hours of their day, and they haven't yet performed a single task that they will be asked to perform on the actual bar exam.

But not you! You are too damn smart for that. You're not going to spend hours each day in class. You're not wasting your time doing busywork that doesn't prepare you for the bar exam, such as reading outlines. Instead, you are going to be practicing actual bar exam tasks by performing them. Doing this will cause you to learn the law so much faster!

The reason you learn the law so much faster this way is because any knowledge gaps become very apparent as you try to write your essay answer. When you come upon a knowledge gap, writing the essay becomes a struggle.

For example, you might try writing a Contracts essay only to realize you are struggling to do an offer and acceptance analysis. You have just discovered a knowledge gap! Be glad when this happens! *It is so much better to uncover that gap now than on the actual bar exam.* You may have thought you knew offer and acceptance. After all, what 2L doesn't? However, understanding the concept in your brain is different from demonstrating that knowledge in bar exam format.

Your brain works harder, and differently, when taking the bar exam. If you don't know - really know - the material being tested, you will become keenly aware of your knowledge gap immediately. But only if you're practicing! Practicing illuminates your knowledge gaps.

If you're reading a flashcard or outline, you will mistakenly believe you know the material. But when you write an essay and find out you don't know offer and acceptance, then it will get cemented into your brain through this process because you must grapple with it while trying to write out your answer. Your brain must work hard to draw upon some knowledge that isn't there, so when you read that rule of law afterward, your brain soaks it up and files away that information so you won't ever have to feel that awful struggle again. Now you will know the rule, and if for some reason it doesn't get cemented in at this point, it only takes one or two more tries until you have it solidly in your memory banks.

Let's say you had been reading an outline instead of doing a practice essay. Would you have tested yourself to see if you could recite the rule of law, out loud, before you read it? Let's give you the benefit of the doubt and say you had taken those steps to test yourself only to find out you couldn't articulate the rule. It's not a big deal, is it? You can just read the rule a second later.

But it's not the same when your entire essay is riding on this key issue. If you can't put the operant rule of law down on paper and then properly analyze the facts, your whole essay is shit. You may only get a few points on the essay, which would make it extremely hard to pass the bar exam.

This type of pressure isn't present when you are just reading through an outline. That is why you will never learn as much by reading outlines as you will by testing yourself. Moreover, that is why doing practice essays will work much, much faster than rote memorization. When you do practice essays and performance tests, you are essentially creating a "sink or swim" or "trial by fire" situation. This raises the stakes and makes your efforts much more effective.

I hope I've driven home how important it is to practice doing the exact tasks that you will be asked to do on the bar exam. It truly is crucial, despite the fact that it deviates from the standard approach that you will probably see most of your friends taking. There is a good reason for this approach, and it truly works.

This approach may sound like more work (and harder work), and it may seem like there is a lazier, more passive option out there. But the truth is, once you get going, you will find that this is actually a lot easier than you thought it would be. You learn <u>faster</u> and more <u>effectively</u>. And not to be dismissed as inconsequential is the **incredible amount of confidence** you will gain in the process. For example, if you follow the approach outlined in this book, you will have written out every essay that has been tested on the bar exam in the last ten years. The numbers vary depending on your jurisdiction, but it will be at least 100 essays. You will also take over 1,200 MBEs.

Can you imagine how much confidence you will have when you walk into the bar exam with 100 essays and 1,200 MBEs under your belt? Do you think you will be worried about your performance? Will you be afraid that you won't know what is going to be tested? Hell no! The confidence you will have on the bar exam will be invaluable. There won't be anything on that bar exam you're not equipped to handle, and feeling that level of preparedness is something you can't buy.

Every. single. day. you will be actively working to improve your bar exam performance. NOTHING you do will be a waste of time or effort. Everything you do will have a direct impact on your performance because it will be something that moves the needle. You have only one goal: to pass the bar exam and claim your seat at counsel table. If you find yourself engaged in any activity which is not in direct alignment with that goal, stop! Just stop. And then get back on task.

———

When I started law school, I was working full time during the day and was enrolled in the evening program, which meant that I didn't get to take Evidence or Civil Procedure my first year like 1Ls usually do. Not having taken Evidence didn't stop me from wanting to participate in a mock trial competition, though! My trial partner (also in the evening program) and I were supposed to be paired against another 1L team. An error was made, and for our very first mock trial, we were pitted against 2Ls who had not only taken Evidence but also had an entire extra year of law school under their belt along with a summer's worth of practical legal experience.

It was a massacre.

We had no idea what we were doing. We didn't know when to make objections, what to object to, how to correctly ask a non-leading question, or even how to cross-examine. It was an extremely painful, stressful, and embarrassing situation. But! We were learning from each mistake we were making. We were learning the hard way, but oh were we learning!

After the blood bath, we regrouped, evaluated the destruction, and re-assessed our trial skills before the next round the following morning. That morning, we were placed against another 1L team for the second round. This 1L team was in the day program, so they still had more legal knowledge than we did due to their Evidence class. However, we had learned a hell of a lot the night before and were confident in our new skills. We creamed them and were advanced to the next round.

It just so happens that we advanced on to face the same exact 2L team we had competed against the night before when we had been mistakenly mismatched. But this time, things were different. Really different. We knew what to do this time. We realized that they had been getting away with murder the night before because of our lack of knowledge. When they tried the same tactics this time, we shut them down. Over and over again. I was even able to get their most hostile witness to impeach himself on the stand. Twenty-four hours previously, I couldn't even get him to talk.

We beat them, and the look on their faces was priceless. It is one of my favorite law school memories. They were completely shocked not only that we were winning, but that we were the same team they had humiliated the night before. We were badass.

Even though we felt completely humiliated and were defeated the previous night, we learned more through that short struggle than we would have in an entire year of a trial skills class. Why? Because we weren't listening to lectures about how a trial works, how to object, how to preserve the record, how to claim privilege, etc. Nor were we observing other people perform a trial and taking mental notes from the safety of the gallery. Both of these techniques are passive ways of learning. Instead, we learned by doing - and that type of learning is the best kind.

6

THE KLEIN METHOD

T his is a point of demarcation in the book. I know that what you've read up until this point has been unorthodox. From the shocking and irreverent title to my complete rejection of almost every single thing that has become known as traditional bar prep (reading outlines, listening to lectures, memorizing mnemonics, etc.), I do things differently. I think for myself, I question the norms, and I follow the outcomes.

So far I have laid out my general bar exam philosophy, or bar exam world view, as it were. This is the general theory about bar prep from which I operate. I have (hopefully) challenged some ideas you had about how difficult the exam is, whether the traditional way of studying makes sense, what actually matters when it comes to passing, and what actions get you ready for the bar. This is information that is helpful to anyone taking the bar exam and provides solid principles to keep in mind regardless of how you ultimately decide to prepare for the bar.

Now, however, we're taking a hard segue. <u>How</u> I go about implementing these core tenets into an actual study approach, and translate my theory into a daily action plan that results in passing the bar, is something else altogether. It is called The Klein Method. Let me introduce you to it.

————

I first developed my method in 2008 when I graduated from law school and was self-studying for the California bar exam. Although I had been a student for twenty years, I had never prepared for any test the way that I decided to prepare for the bar exam. Since the bar exam was a new kind of test for me, I needed a new kind of approach. I began piecing it together as I was struggled to find my way self-studying. Little by little I added steps, removed time-wasters, tweaked my approach, and found a way to systematize and organize everything so I had momentum, structure, and was progressing. I was creating a unique study approach for the bar exam, from scratch.

Through that process, despite all the speed bumps and hiccups along the way, I found that my study approach was incredibly effective. Not only was it really easy to do, it was also very powerful. I used it to pass the California Bar Exam. A few years later I moved to Virginia and again used it to self-study and pass that bar exam.

I have been sharing my method on a small scale for years, and in the last couple years even began coaching people through bar prep using it. I have seen lots of people pass using The Klein Method when traditional methods failed them.

I have not stopped tweaking and perfecting it over the years, either. Although the core of The Klein Method has never changed, the smaller details have morphed as I see more and more people use it and receive additional data and feedback.

[For example, as you will read in a later chapter, one aspect of The Klein Method is that I break down bar prep into 80 4-hour Study Blocks, for a total of 320 hours of studying. However, the results I've seen from students is that some people have fallen behind and done less than 80 Study Blocks, yet still passed the bar exam. That causes me to consider whether all 80 Study Blocks are necessary, or if doing only 60 or 70 Study Blocks will provide the same result. One day I might determine that The Klein Method only requires 65 Study Blocks and tweak my program to reflect that change, but the use of the 4-hour Study Block is a core and foundational principle of The Klein Method that shall remain.]

I'm about to tell you about another one of the foundational principles of The Klein Method, that I first developed and implemented back in 2008. It is called the 4 Stages, and in the following chapter I explain what those are and show you how to use them. The 4 Stages require the application of a special technique. Out of curiosity, when preparing to write the first edition of this book, I decided to do some research and see if the technique I used is "a thing" or happened to have a name.

It turns out, the technique *is* a thing, and it also has a name (which I will discuss shortly). And yet, the way in which I applied that technique and the methods I developed were uniquely my own. It was clear that I had blazed a new trail in the bar prep space all those years ago when I first put together my novel and powerful system of preparation.

Before I jump into telling you about the technique, I want to give you a brief preface so that you have a framework with which to understand the concept of it. Because I know that it is a very unusual approach to the bar exam, allow me to defend it before you decide whether to give it any credence.

The bar exam is writing heavy. We all know this. Depending on what jurisdiction you are taking, you will likely have two written portions: essays and performance tests. Your writing skill is of utmost importance in getting every point you can. As we already established, your writing is the medium by which you connect with the bar grader and demonstrate your legal knowledge and competence. It is the only way that you can jump off the page and shout: "*Hey! I'm brilliant and will be a great attorney. I deserve a seat at counsel table.*"

You want to make it *as easy as possible* for the grader to get that message. It's your responsibility to send that message loud and clear. If the grader doesn't get that message when they read your answer, that's on you. The bar examiners have already done all they can to help you. They published all the earlier tests and told you how to answer them well by publishing the selected answers. It's practically been handed to you on a silver platter.

The best way to utilize that invaluable information and use it to your bar exam benefit is to *copy model answers*. No, I'm not talking about *emulating* them or *modeling* your answer after them. I mean to *literally copy them*. Word for word. Over and over again, until you have created a well-worn map in your brain about how to write a high-scoring essay or performance test answer.

As I discovered, this technique of copying good writing is a practice called "copywork." Turns out, it is centuries old. It is used to educate and to improve writing, and it is all but forgotten these days, although its use can still be found in some homeschool circles following the Charlotte Mason method (Charlotte Mason was a famous liberal educator at the turn of the 20th century).

I learned that some famous writers used copywork, including Jack London, Robert Louis Stevenson, and Benjamin Franklin. I also found a modern reference to the technique. Art of Manliness writer Brett McKay shares how he used copywork in law school as a way to improve his writing:

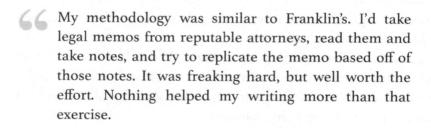

> My methodology was similar to Franklin's. I'd take legal memos from reputable attorneys, read them and take notes, and try to replicate the memo based off of those notes. It was freaking hard, but well worth the effort. Nothing helped my writing more than that exercise.

When I uncovered this information in my research, years after I had been independently employing this technique as one part of my overall method, and realized that not only was it a thing called copywork, but that it had been historically proven to be reliable, I was really excited to have my intuition and study method validated.

You should be excited too, because as I am about to tell you the amazing results you can get from using the technique in the unique way that I show you, you can be confident that this technique isn't just anecdotally effective.

Copying model answers has a number of incredible benefits which are not all immediately apparent. The power behind employing this technique in the way that I will be teaching you to do in the next chapter is actually somewhat staggering.

BENEFIT #1: IT MAKES IT EASY TO GET STARTED

The first benefit of copying model answers is how helpful this process is to getting going. Cracking open your laptop and looking at the blank document in front of you is no fun. This is why people put it off as long as possible! Getting started can be so hard to do. It's incredible how many things need cleaning, how many errands need running, how many emails need answering, and how many groceries need buying. Is your dental cleaning or oil change overdue? Better knock that out today so you can focus all your attention on bar prep *tomorrow*. Procrastination is a real challenge.

However, if all you have to do is simply copy what someone else already wrote, it's not so bad. It's not so hard to sit down and open your computer. You know exactly what you need to put into that blank document because it's already been done for you, so it doesn't even seem like work. You aren't yet at the stage where you're struggling through writing an essay answer on your own. You are riding the coattails of someone who has already done it (and done it well). So before you know it, you've gotten started. And at the end of the day, you see that you've copied five essays! The next day, five more. By the end of two weeks, you've copied fifty essays! Fifty!! Moreover, you didn't even break a sweat.

There's a reason that you put off practicing essays and performance tests. There's a reason you want to click play on that lecture or the YouTube tutorial. There's a reason you want to flip through some flashcards, read an outline, or answer a few MBEs on that app... Because writing an essay is hard! It takes a long period of complete focus and concentration. It requires you to *truly know* the subject matter and create a written product that 100% came from your own brain.

But what if all those things were no longer true? What if you could actually start knocking out some essays without all that struggle? What if you could get all the benefits of practicing essays without all the difficulties of practicing essays? Wouldn't it be easier to get yourself to simply... START?

That's precisely what copying model answers does - it gets you started. Once you start, you gain momentum and confidence and incentive to keep moving forward, which is obviously the right direction.

You've heard it said that the workout you *do* do, no matter how short, is better than the workout you *don't* do. It's the same here. Consider this a micro goal - one that is almost *too easy* and which guarantees your success. Everyone likes to engage in an activity that they can be successful at. The simplicity of copying a model answer gives you that immediate, easy, and rewarding win that will start you on the path to bar exam readiness.

BENEFIT #2: YOU QUICKLY DISCOVER THE TESTING PATTERNS

If you are in a jurisdiction which uses 30-minutes essays, and you spend a normal 8-hour study day copying model answers, you will be able to copy sixteen essays <u>in one day</u>. Let's say you study a very conservative 40-hours per week. That equates to eighty essays <u>in one week</u>. EIGHTY. Now let's assume you do this for a mere six weeks. The math is simple: 480 essays. <u>480</u>. That would be the equivalent of going through every single essay question that has been tested in the last twenty years (forty administrations of the bar exam), *twice*.

Can you see how this adds up? Even if you're in a 60-minute essay jurisdiction like California and have to cut those numbers in half, you're still talking about massive amounts of essays over the course of a few weeks. (And since I've just finished explaining how *easy* this is to do, the thought of spending an 8-hour study day doing essays should not scare you, make you groan, or cause you to feel dread in the least.)

Guess what happens when you go through large amounts of past essays like this? You are going to see - really, really quickly - that there are patterns to the essays. The bar examiners ask the same things over and over again. There is a very clearly defined 20% of the law that gets tested 80% of the time. Pareto's principle is alive and well here. For example, in California, the subject of Professional Responsibility has been tested on every single exam in the past ten years except once (as of the date of this writing). That's nineteen out of the last twenty administrations. Torts has only been tested eight times during that same period.

Now let's say you were taking the traditional approach and spent your 8-hour study day working on Professional Responsibility and Torts. You spent four hours reading the Professional Responsibility outline, and four hours reading the Torts outline. You will have just spent equal time on subjects that are tested (and therefore weighted) unequally.

When you spend your time more wisely by going through past essays, you will not only learn what the bar graders test, you will automatically be spending proportionate amounts of time on those subjects.

BENEFIT #3: YOU LEARN WHICH ARE THE HIGHLY TESTED ISSUES

Closely related to discovering for yourself what the testing patterns of the bar examiners are, is discovering the highly tested issues within those subjects. It will become so incredibly clear to you what the important legal principles are for each and every subject. The black letter law that *actually gets tested* is going to be popping up over and over again.

If you spent four hours reading a Torts outline, you would be spending the same amount of time on all aspects of Torts. This is the inverse of Pareto's principle! What a waste of your limited time! If you did it the traditional way, not only would you not know the highly tested issues better than the infrequently tested issues, you wouldn't even know what the highly tested issues <u>are</u>!

However, if you were doing essays during those four hours, you would know that out of the eight Torts essays you just did, five of them tested negligence, two of them tested products liability, and one of them tested assault and battery. Now *that's* useful information that will actually make you more ready to perform well on the bar exam.

Torts outlines don't list negligence five times in a row, products liability two times in a row, and assault and battery once (while also eliminating all the untested issues) so that you are spending your time proportionately and focusing on the areas where you will be able to gain most points.

But if you spend your time copying model answers, you will be spending your time proportionately and capitalizing on your score by focusing on where the points are. You will see that some issues are outliers which are tested infrequently. Some issues are never tested. When you have seen every essay question that has been tested in your state for the last ten, fifteen, or twenty years, you will have a very secure grasp on what black letter law you need to know to be ready for the exam.

Benefit #4: You Learn Effortlessly by Deconstruction

By copying sample answers, you learn a whole hell of a lot. It's a practice that confers its benefit through the process of doing it. You will never do anything with the essays or performance tests once you've copied them. The act of copying them was the point. When you copy the sample answers, word for word, sentence for sentence, and paragraph for paragraph, you are learning a ton. I referenced the adage "practice makes perfect" earlier, but the better adage is "perfect practice makes perfect."

When you're doing copywork, and your fingers are busy typing out the sample answer in front of you, your brain is quietly at work in the background deconstructing the well-written sample answer. As it does, you learn how to:

- Identify the legal issues raised by the call of the question;

- Identify which issues are major and require significant time/analysis;

- Identify which issues are minor and can be quickly mentioned/dismissed;

- Cull the appropriate facts from the question and use them in your answer;

- Apply the facts to the law and present a thorough, well thought out analysis;

- Best organize the answer, especially for complex or confusing calls, or in cross-over questions;

- Transition smoothly and logically between issues;

- Conclude succinctly;

- Sound lawyerly by using the proper tone and vocabulary;

- Formulate good rule statements;

- Determine what the heavily tested areas are by seeing which issues show up over and over again;

- Determine what legal issues are not important because they either never show up or show up very rarely;

- Methodically format your answer by using writing cues such as: Under, Here, Therefore;

- Visually lead the grader with good use of paragraph breaks, underscores, headers, etc.;

- Write well with simple, logical, and effective sentences; and

- Make a persuasive legal argument.

BENEFIT #5: YOU AVOID COMMON PITFALLS

Not only are you learning what to do, but you are also learning what not to do, which is just as important. So instead of writing practice essays on your own and solidifying any bad habits you may have, you can avoid them altogether.

This is especially true if you have taken the bar exam one or more times before. If this is your situation, you probably have some entrenched writing habits. Poor writing habits. Unless and until you correct them, you will continue to reinforce them. Some bad habits you will avoid by copying sample answers include:

- Overlooking issues

- Including irrelevant issues;

- Wasting time on minor issues;

- Mis-stating rule statements;

- Missing important analysis;

- Rambling;

- Disorganization;

- Floundering during transitions;

- Failing to conclude; and

- Being conclusory (this is a huge one!)

BENEFIT #6: YOU WILL "CRACK THE CODE"

As you continue to copy model answers, you will realize that your brain has started to think the same way. You will begin to anticipate what a model answer should look like and sound like. As you read an essay question legal issues start jumping out at you from the fact pattern, which likely was already happening before you started copying model answers since law school already trained you to think that way and to spot them. But now, unlike before, what also starts happening without any additional effort is that you will start "writing" the essay answer in your head automatically or anticipate (accurately) how the model answer will be structured, what the rule statements are, how it will be organized, etc.

You basically begin to know what a model answer will look like before you even read it. When this happens, you have reached your goal because you will start writing just like the model answers. And as we already know, those answers are high scoring and well-written. Essentially what you've done when this happens is "crack the code." You will know when it happens. You just "get it" on a level you didn't before. You see the essays differently. *It all makes sense.*

This level of familiarity with this portion of the exam, its structure, and understanding what the bar graders wish to see in a passing answer is a critical shift and skill you acquire when you copy model answer after model answer.

BENEFIT #7: FOREIGN ATTORNEYS BECOME "AMERICANIZED"

One benefit that would never have occurred to me if I hadn't started coaching is how copying model answers helps foreign examinees. As a born and bred American who went to a U.S. law school, the unique challenges of taking the bar exam as a foreigner had never crossed my mind.

Then I started getting contacted by foreign-trained examinees, who were concerned about their disadvantage. Some were barred in another country and took open-book bar exams. Understandably, they felt intimidated about taking the bar exam in the U.S. My hat comes off to them, as I am truly impressed by their ambition to become licensed in an entirely new country.

The first thing foreigners need to know is that they are no less intelligent than their American counterparts and if the Americans can pass the exam, so can they.

In the end, *everyone* is taking the *same* test. The benefits of applying this approach are just as effective for foreigners as they are for Americans.

The particular benefit that foreign examinees receive from copying model answers that extends beyond all the other benefits I've been discussing, is they will get a boost in learning American English on a deeper level. From little things like how Americans spell some words differently than other forms of English, to conjugating verbs properly, they will be flooded with practice in how to sound more American and more like the other examinees.

Traditional bar prep doesn't inundate foreign examinees in writing like copying model answers does. Using this strategy will naturally improve their mastery of our language along the way by default.

BENEFIT #8: YOU'LL NEVER HAVE TO MEMORIZE

Traditionally, the last week or two of bar prep is devoted to rote memorization of black letter law (BLL), mnemonics, attack sheets, and other such material. Bar preppers who haven't been practicing essays very much don't trust themselves to know what they need to know come exam day. They are trying to jam it all into their brains so that it will stick in there just long enough to take the exam before it all tumbles out of their gray matter.

That is a reality that simply doesn't exist for the person who uses this approach for one simple reason: you *already know* all the BLL that you need. That 20% of the law you have been spending 100% of your time on, has been so thoroughly covered that it found a permanent home in your brain without any additional memorization sessions.

Here's why.

You have gone through hundreds of essays, which have covered a finite number of legal issues and black letter rules. Those finite number of rules have popped up over and over and over and over again (patterns, remember?), so you have been repeating them all along. The repetition already happened through frequency. But it gets better...

When you copy a model answer, you are engaging with the BLL multiple times. The first "hit," as it were, is when you read the BLL in the model essay (visual). The second "hit" is when you type or handwrite the BLL as you copy the model answer (physical). The third "hit" is when you see the BLL that you just typed or wrote (visual). And I am willing to bet that if you are like most people, as you copy something you are also saying it to yourself so that you can get the wording just right and don't forget it from one moment to another (let's call this auditory). That's the fourth "hit." A bonus fifth "hit" is if you are a mumbler and actually say it to yourself, out loud, as you copy it because then you are hearing it with your ears as well as your inner voice.

Can you see how copying a model answer gives you a good three to five neurological imprints of the BLL?

When you are reading an outline, or watching a lecture, or going through a flashcard, you are engaging with the BLL once, by reading. You might decide to say it to yourself, or say it out loud, which is better and gives you a second "hit." But even so, you aren't getting the same bang for your buck.

Another way in which this approach helps you memorize effortlessly is because you've been *engaging* the BLL through essays and seeing it work *in action*. Having this context is like a hook in your brain; it allows you to grasp the material in a more meaningful way and to remember it more easily. You haven't been trying to jam the BLL into your brain through rote memorization from a boring list on a piece of paper or from a flashcard.

Lastly, what you have been memorizing (without effort) by copying model answers is not competing with lots of other legal rules that you don't need to know for the bar exam. You have essentially culled 80% of the legal principles that you might otherwise spend trying to jam into your memory banks in the last two weeks of prep.

BENEFIT #9: YOU WILL BE CONFIDENT!

When you start copying model essay answers and spend your time practicing essays as opposed to reading outlines, watching lectures, and the like, you gain an indescribable amount of confidence. The kind of confidence that changes the game altogether.

Imagine for a moment that you have fast forwarded in time and suddenly you are sitting in the bar exam, looking at your computer, and the proctors are about to begin the exam. If you have walked into that bar exam and have read every single essay question that has been asked on the bar exam in the last twenty years - along with a model answer - will you feel worried about what might be lurking in that pack of test papers you are about to open?

Fuck. No.

What about if you've "only" gone through the last ten years? I bet you're still feeling pretty fucking confident in that moment.

There's simply no alternative to the confidence you get from following this approach. None whatsoever. It doesn't matter if you had a bar grader tutor you. It doesn't matter if you spent more money on bar prep than anyone else in the history of the country. Nothing compares to walking in, sitting down, and *knowing* from the deepest part of yourself, that you are READY. It's what happens when you know that not only is there a less than 5% chance that something will show up that you haven't seen after all that practice, *but even if it does*, you know how to handle it like a boss. Worst case scenario, if you don't know the rule for an outlier issue being tested and have to improvise, it won't derail your strong performance on every other part of the test and *will not* jeopardize your outcome.

When you walk into the bar exam *like that*, you are sitting pretty.

When you walk through bar <u>prep</u> *like that*, you have already won.

Confidence is a big deal. My first entire chapter was devoted to trying to remind you who you are and that you already have good reason to be confident. Feeling confident in your preparation is an important component of performing well on bar exam day. But feeling confident in your study plan is important *every day*. When you copy model answers, and when you start writing your own essay answers (to be discussed later), you develop more confidence every day. You will *know* that when you close your computer at the end of your study session that you are more ready to take the bar exam than you were when you opened your computer at the beginning of your study session. The same cannot be said if your study session consisted of reading outlines.

When you are preparing for the bar exam and you do not feel confident, you end up walking around with a certain level of mental torment. It's exhausting. You're worried and stressed all the time. You feel overwhelmed and panicked because you constantly doubt whether you're doing enough, whether you're good enough, improving enough, know enough, studying enough, enough, enough, enough...

It becomes a negative and demoralizing cycle. The incessant doubts strip you of your energy. In order to combat the worries, you spend hours and hours doing more of the same thinking (hoping) that by sheer volume you will do "enough" to pass. Or you start combing the web looking for new study materials or a new study plan or a new training to buy because you think that maybe if you buy that book, or attack sheet, or outline, or training that it will hold the key to passing the bar exam.

When you are doing <u>effective</u> work, you know it. No one has to tell you. No one has to explain it to you. No one has to reassure you.

You feel settled and confident. *You know*, and that makes you confident.

BENEFIT #10: YOU WILL FEEL LESS STRESS

Closely related to the confidence you will experience is the benefit of having a drastic reduction in stress. You already understand the weight that comes along with this process. It's that 800-pound gorilla that follows you around and torments you at all hours of the day and night. It hangs on you and weighs you down. It's inescapable. Or is it?

Something magical happens to that gorilla when you start copying model answers as I describe. At the end of each study day, when you have made *real*, *meaningful*, and *effective* progress, and when you see how today's work is part of an overall study system which will truly have you ready to excel on the bar exam, then you can close your laptop at the end of the day feeling <u>accomplished</u>, <u>proud</u>, and <u>relaxed</u>.

Whatever you want to do after you close your laptop, you can do - *without stress*. You no longer feel:

- anxiety that you "should be" studying more,

- worry that you aren't doing the "right things" that will get you ready,

- dread about how quickly the bar exam is approaching on the calendar,

- guilt any time you spend time doing anything other than studying

- racing thoughts when you're lying in bed trying to sleep

When you've closed your laptop after an honest day's work and feel confident about the progress you made, you can turn off that part of your brain and your life (the "bar exam" part) and actually re-engage the remaining parts of your life. You can do all sorts of things you want to without the constant stress and anxiety that used to plague you. Whether that's going out to a bar, seeing a movie, spending time with your boyfriend/girlfriend, playing with your children, going for a hike, attending your cousin's wedding over the weekend... whatever it is you want to do you can now do without stress because you've already handled the bar exam part of your life in a way that you feel confident in and which makes you feel accomplished.

These are the types of life activities that help you stay connected to loved ones, stay balanced and healthy, and make life maintainable. When you can engage in them without worrying about the bar exam in the back of your mind the entire time, and are truly present, then those activities will reenergize, relax, and nurture you. Being able to decompress through these activities further de-stresses you and now you are in a healthy cycle of relaxation and rejuvenation instead of an unhealthy cycle of increasing stress and anxiety.

Imagine what that feels like on a typical bar prep study day... you wake up and study at the law library from 9 a.m. to 6 p.m. (you've taken a full hour for lunch and study breaks). You've done 50 MBEs and 12 essays during your eight hour study day. You get in an hour at the gym on your way home, from 6 p.m. to 7 p.m., then have a healthy dinner from 7 p.m. to 8 p.m. You decide to go out and see the newest comedy flic with your bestie, and laugh your ass off. You're home and in bed by 11 p.m. and fall right asleep. You haven't given the bar exam any thought since you closed your laptop at 6 p.m. because you feel great about the progress you made and know you are right on track. You sleep soundly a full 8 hours and wake refreshed and ready to hit the books again in the morning. Rinse and repeat.

Can you see how this type of bar prep lifestyle reduces your stress? It's a cycle that begets further and increased benefits, and it all starts with the confidence you get from truly doing meaningful and effective work with your study hours. There's no way that you can do

12 essays and 50 MBEs in a single study day and walk away after 8 hours feeling anxious about whether you "did enough," "know enough," worked "hard enough," or will be "ready enough." It's just not possible to do this day in and day out, week in and week out, and not see your confidence skyrocket, which, in turn, causes your stress levels to plummet.

This positive and uplifting snowball effect is simply a natural benefit of this approach. And the better it gets, the better it gets, because what happens when you reduce your stress is that your brain works even better for you. A brain that is well-rested and healthy can absorb and recall more information, as well as focus for longer periods of time. This makes your study periods more effective, your memory stronger, and your performance improve - all great things when you want to pass the bar exam.

7

THE 4 STAGES

T he technique of copywork, and the benefits of it which I just discussed at length in the previous chapter, is only one aspect of The Klein Method, which encompasses a much broader strategy of preparing for the bar exam.

Copying model answers is only the first of a four stage process that gets you ready to excel on the written portion of the bar exam. Despite how powerful copying model answers is, and how many amazing benefits it confers, at some point it must transition into you being able to write *your own* essay answers and performance tests since that is what you must do on exam day.

Thus, copying model answers is only Stage 1, which begins your journey and gets you off to a very strong start and equips you with what you need to succeed as you progress.

After Stage 1 comes Stage 2, in which you'll make a small change. The transition will seem minor and totally do-able, so it won't seem too bad or trigger procrastination. Plus, you've already copied dozens of essays, so you already have the hang of it and are in the flow. You have momentum behind you making it much easier. After that is Stage 3, with another slight change, then Stage 4, where you will be writing essays with no training wheels and absolutely crushing bar prep! This unique process is designed to build on your earlier successes and easily ramp you up to bar exam day.

STAGE 2 - THE EYE-OPENER

Stage 2 is just like Stage 1 with one difference: after you've read the question and copied the model answer, you will put away the model answer and write your own answer. This stage will be the most eye-opening for you. This is where you will be shocked at just how different it is to read an answer versus write an answer.

If the distinction between passive learning and active practice hadn't been made clear before, it will be driven home when you enter this stage. You will likely think you know so much about writing answers (and indeed you will have learned a lot by now), but you will be surprised by how it's not as easy to write an essay as you thought, even though you just copied one!

It is imperative to move on to this next stage even if you don't feel ready yet. In fact, it is *expected* that you will feel as though you don't know enough of the law (or don't know it well enough yet) to begin doing practice essays on your own. Like I discussed earlier, this is precisely why you need to start writing essays now.

It is the struggle that catapults you to quickly becoming very good at writing essays. Waiting until you "feel ready" is the kiss of death for bar prep. There is so much material you will never feel completely ready. The act of writing essays is what gets the content in your head and makes you feel ready.

It bears repeating that as you practice writing essays, you will learn what the core set of material is for each subject. Certain issues will be repeated continually, and the information you thought you had to have memorized before you could even start writing essays will appear in your memory banks as if by magic.

The other material, which only pops up now and again on the essays, are not the major issues. You will spend less time on them because they are tested infrequently, and this is how it ought to be. You should not be spending equal time on material that has unequal weight. As you spend your time doing practice exams, this sorts itself out naturally.

The logistics of this stage are as follows: If you are in a jurisdiction with sixty minute essays, you should aim to spend approximately forty-five minutes reading the question and copying the sample answer. Then you will spend another forty-five minutes drafting your own answer. Remember you will have already read the question and copied the model answer, so that shaves off about fifteen minutes of work when it's time for you to write your own answer. Since you didn't have to spend the brainpower to organize and think through an answer when you first read the question and copied the model, it should only have taken you about forty-five minutes for that portion as well.

If you are in a jurisdiction with thirty minute essays, you will spend approximately forty-five minutes total: half the time should be used to read and copy; half to write your own answer.

STAGE 3 - THE FLIP FLOP

Stage 3 is just like Stage 2 with one difference: after you've read the question, you will write your own answer first, and then copy the model answer. You simply flip-flop the order in which you work through each essay.

As you can probably imagine, this slight change will hoist you from one level to an entirely new level. Your proficiency will be significantly improved.

During this stage, you must really make a 100% effort each and every time you write an essay. Don't give up if you can't recall the applicable rule of law. If you know there's a rule, but can't remember it exactly, do your very best to take the general idea and formulate your own rule.

Pushing through when your brain is frantically trying to recall its legal knowledge is what will make the rule really stick when you copy the model answer afterward. Not to mention you might have the unlucky fortune of facing a similar situation on the real bar exam. If a minor point of law is tested for the first time in fifteen years, and you only vaguely remember the rule from one of your law school classes or outline, you will need to know how to deal with that situation elegantly.

The logistics of this stage are as follows: If you are in a jurisdiction with sixty minute essays, you will spend sixty minutes reading the question and writing your answer. Then you will spend about another thirty minutes copying the model answer. If you are in a jurisdiction with thirty minute essays, you will spend thirty minutes reading the question and writing your answer. Then you will spend another fifteen minutes copying the model answer.

A word on timing: stick to the limit imposed by your jurisdiction, whether thirty or sixty minutes. Hordes of examinees run out of time on the essays because they use too much time on the earlier essays and set themselves up for failure in the last essay. Do NOT get in the bad habit of giving yourself any extra time. Be immovable on this rule.

Each essay question has been written so that it may be sufficiently answered in the time allotted. Unless you have some individual circumstance which causes you to require more time and have received an accommodation from the bar examiners, you should be completing your essays in that time frame.

If you are consistently running out of time, you are probably writing more rule statements than necessary, spending too much time on minor issues, or "finding" too many issues to discuss (don't throw the kitchen sink in there).

Also extremely important is not allowing yourself to peek at the answer. Do NOT get into this terrible habit. You need to be treating the practice essay like an actual exam because on the real exam, you will have no crutch - no notes to lean on when the going gets tough. Just get used to it right now, and save yourself a lot of trouble later on when it truly counts.

Similarly, make sure your email is closed, your phone is silenced, there's no music playing in the background, etc. Silence all notifications, use the Do Not Disturb setting on your technology, or whatever it takes to remove all distractions. Get used to the sound of your keyboard and your thoughts. That's all you need. Keep building your mental stamina and improving your concentration. The only things in front of you should be your computer and the essay question.

If you've already downloaded the exam software, use it for some of your practice essays. There are quite a few tools on the toolbar which are useful if you are familiar enough to employ them. For example, you can set a timer that you can use to notify you when you're almost out of time. This is invaluable if you continually struggle to keep an eye on your time or run out of time.

After you've written your essay answer on your own and copied the model answer, make mental notes of the differences. Here are some things you should be taking notice of as you copy the model answer (which your brain is probably automatically doing for you anyway):

ORGANIZATION

- How is the model answer organized? When does it use headers? What do the headers look like?

- Does your essay visually look the same or similar?

- What does the overall formatting of the model look like? Are there lots of paragraph breaks and space between sections? Is it easy on the eye and does it draw the grader's attention?

- Does your answer look readable or is it a large mass of unending text?

- On questions that include multiple parties, how did the sample handle them? By issue or by party? Was your essay organized/planned the same way?

- Did your essay waste time by repeating entire issues/analyses which could have been consolidated for multiple parties?

- On cross-over questions, which subjects/issues did the model address first? Was your essay as logical and organized? Would the grader be able to follow your organization easily, or become confused or lost?

ISSUE

- What issues does the model address?

- Did you miss any?

- Did you add irrelevant issues to your essay?

- Do your issue headers clearly show the grader what issue will be addressed next? Do they provide a roadmap to your analysis?

RULE

- How does the model essay formulate the rule statements?

- What rule statements were included in the model?

- How were they organized if there were multiple rules or long/complex rules?

- Were they organized well?

- Did you include rule statements that were irrelevant or superfluous?

ANALYSIS

- What facts did the model rely on in the analysis?

- How did the model go about applying the facts to the law?

- Did you miss important cues in the essay questions that the bar examiners included by the use of specific facts?

- Did you fully develop your analysis by applying the facts to the rule, or were you conclusory?

CONCLUSION

- Were the conclusions in the model unambiguous and efficient?

- What was the transition like from one conclusion to the next issue/section?

- Were you able to succinctly wrap up analyses with an effective conclusion and logically move on to the next section?

If your essays look and sound like an incomprehensible mess compared to the model answer, I have lots of good news for you!

First, it is expected that they will, especially when you're just getting started. Writing bar exam essay answers is its own art form. They are not like exams you took in law school, where your professor enjoyed reading all the theoretical and public policy arguments you could think of. They are not like any other types of essays you've ever written, either. Do not become discouraged when you see the stark difference between your essay and the model essay. It is normal. Remember, this is precisely why you are copying the sample answers - you are learning the art form by copying the masters, as it were.

Second, if your essay doesn't sound or look like the model, that means you see the differences between the two. It would be of concern if you couldn't pick up on the distinctions. However, since you can see exactly what is different, you know what you need to change and are equipped to make those changes next time. With every essay you practice, you become better and better at incorporating all the changes and tweaking your writing skills so that you write like the samples.

The amount of time you stay in this stage is going to be dependent on you and the progress you are making. If while writing your practice essays you can anticipate what the model answer would look like, how it would be organized, etc., and then it does actually look a lot like the model, then you are ready to move on to the next stage.

If there are still some significant differences between your essays and the models, keep working in this stage. If you're finding that there are one or two particular writing skills that you just haven't mastered (such as organization, or avoiding conclusory statements), really sit down with the model answers and study what they do and don't do. Bar exam essay writing isn't a mystery; it's a skill that can be learned as long as you have a requisite level of competency. There are patterns to the essay questions and patterns to good answers. There is certain terminology. Sit down with a bunch of essays and model answers, and note what is the same in each essay. What is repeated? What patterns are you finding? Once you find them (and you will), employ them.

If you think this is too much work, remember that we are going for quality, not merely quantity. Quantity will come naturally if you're making sure to practice essays every day. However, if you're not putting in the necessary effort, it doesn't matter how many you do. You need to learn how to write good answers. So really pay attention to the model answers and continue to deconstruct their attributes as you go along. They are the answer key to this portion of the bar exam. As you spend time copying model answers, how they are written will be imprinted on your brain and available for recall when you sit for the exam.

STAGE 4 - THE FULL MONTY

In the last stage, you continue taking practice exams, just like in Stage 3. Now, however, instead of copying the model answer afterward, simply read through it. What you want to be doing is basically skimming the model to check your own answer against. You already know how to write a good answer, so you're just checking to see if you missed any issues, organized the answer correctly, etc.

If you find that you messed up somehow, again just make a mental note of what the model answer did compared to what you did. You should be able to spot differences pretty easily by now and make the necessary course corrections. It is not necessary to copy the model answers.

When you are practicing in this final stage, if you come across any issues for which you do not know the rule statement, push through and still write your answer as if you had to turn it into the bar graders. However, when you are finished, make sure to look at the rule statement in the model answer (or in an outline if you prefer), so you can add it to your memory banks. Copy the rule statement from the model answer or the outline. Then, close the model answer or outline and try to write the rule statement out again from memory, so you know you have it.

If you employ this strategy and write every essay that has been tested in the last ten, fifteen, or twenty years, it is highly unlikely that many issues will pop up that you don't know, but if that happens, this is how you should approach it so you solidify that legal knowledge in your brain.

8

SOURCING MATERIALS

Where to get practice essays and sample answers is a question you will have to answer if you wish to employ the strategy outlined in this book.

RELEASED SAMPLE ANSWERS

Approximately 42 jurisdictions administer the Multistate Essay Exam (MEE), which is created by the National Conference of Bar Examiners (NCBE). The NCBE provides five years of past MEE Questions and Analyses directly on their website for free. Some of the MEE jurisdictions, such as Minnesota, Arkansas, and New York, also provide questions and sample answers for free on their websites. By going directly to these sources, you can get your hands on plenty of practice materials for free. Links to these sources are available at FckTheBar.com. In California, seven years of prior questions and sample answers are provided. Links to these, plus additional older questions that the State Bar of California has since removed from their website, are also available on the freebies link above.

If you have heard that the released sample answers written from past bar takers are not suitable to use when studying, let me you disabuse you of that idea. The samples that are released have been done so for your benefit. These entities have no other purpose in releasing these samples except to provide transparency and to illustrate to bar examinees what they are looking for in a good answer by showing you an example of one that scored well. They haven't decided to provide just passing answers - they have provided excellent answers.

Let's see what they say about the samples they have selectively chosen to publish:

- California: "The answers were assigned high grades and were written by applicants who passed the examination after one read."

- New York: "The following are sample candidate answers that received scores superior to the average scaled score awarded for the relevant essay ... These answers are intended to demonstrate the general length and quality of responses that earned above-average scores on the indicated administration of the bar examination."

- Minnesota: Minnesota simply titles the released answers as "Representative Good Answers" with no additional details.

- Arkansas: "The top examination paper in each subject shall be available for review... "

It would be disingenuous of me to fail to mention that almost all of these sources also provide disclaimers and warnings, discouraging examinees from relying on these published answers for preparation. This is completely understandable. After all, we're dealing with would-be lawyers and a highly litigious society. Disclaimers are everywhere. Providing information and advice does not guarantee anything. There are no guarantees in life. So you should read the full disclaimers they post for yourself and make your own decisions. Like-wise, after reading this book you should make your own determina-tion about how to study for the bar exam. How you prepare is ultimately on you. No one can take that responsibility from you.

That said, if I were trying to score as many points as possible on the bar exam, you can bet your bottom dollar that I would want to know exactly what the high scoring answers were! Is it more dangerous to use imperfect, but high scoring answers as an example of what the bar examiners are looking for, or to use nothing at all and take some shots in the dark? Is it risky to see what the answers that received high scores contain and how they are written? What if you looked at enough of these top scoring answers to notice commonalities between them? Wouldn't you want to implement those common attributes into your own answers with the intent that you would also score in the same range as those answers did?

COMMERCIAL ANSWERS

An alternate option for getting practice essays and answers is to buy them from commercial sources. Books of them are available on the market, or through different courses, some of which are better known than others. The benefit of such books is that they are nicely compiled and bound for you. They will also have consistent rule statements and organizational flow because they have been produced by one source.

These consistencies can help you learn a little more quickly because of the repetition. For example, if every time you see the rule statement for negligence, it is worded exactly the same, your brain will remember it much faster than if every time you read the state-ment it is worded slightly differently (because it was written by different people).

The same goes for the organization. If every single time you see the IRAC organized the same way (i.e., each conclusion begins with "Therefore," and every section header is underlined) then you will more quickly set a standard procedure for how you organize your own answers.

[There is a distinction between books containing complete essay answers and books which are filled with outlines, or "attack sheets," or the legal rules only. You want to be copying full essay answers. Remember: if it isn't *exactly* what you will have to do on the real bar exam, then you are selling yourself short. You get graded on your performance. If it's not full performance, then you're missing points.]

The downside of commercially prepared books is that they are unlikely to provide each essay tested over the last ten years, so although they might include an essay which tests the issue of negligence, for example, they might not provide essays which test that issue in the same proportion as the bar examiners test it.

If negligence is one of the 20% of legal issues that get tested 80% of the time, but you've only seen it in their book once or twice, you might not be giving it due attention which will be to your detriment. This is a big downside. If you're in California, for example, Professional Responsibility has been tested on every single bar exam in the last ten years except once (that's nineteen out of twenty times!). Torts, on the other hand, has only been tested on about half of the exams. If you have a book that has five Professional Responsibility essays and five Torts essays, you are going to have a problem.

The other downside of using commercial books is that although the answers included in the books are going to be passing answers, they might not have scored as high as the released samples (assuming arguendo that they had also been submitted to the bar graders). Using the released samples is really a commentary from the bar graders essentially saying: "*This. This is what we're looking for.*" The high scoring sample answers released by the bar examiners are superior writing examples which often provide a more sophisticated answer than you will find in the commercial books.

Once you start working with the high scoring samples, you will begin to see the commonalities and patterns which are making those answers high scoring. Their commonalities are more subtle and aren't as initially apparent, whereas commercial answers are blatantly obvious in their commonalities, making them easier to *identify and mimic*. The ability to easily deconstruct and mimic is the benefit of commercial essays.

Make no mistake: the answers you buy in commercially-prepared books will be giving you examples of reliable, proficient, and passing essay answers. However, if you compare a commercial answer to one of the released sample answers, you will see that the commercial answer will be shorter, simpler, and more straightforward. The sample answer will be more lengthy, fluid, and sophisticated.

Commercial answers have a very distinctive and clean IRAC structure that is easier to emulate. Sample answers do more weaving of facts and analyses that reveal a more stylistic approach.

Commercial essay books are like buying a pizza from Pizza Hut. In contrast, released sample answers are like buying a pizza from your local wood-fired restaurant that sources local ingredients. You can go to a Pizza Hut anywhere in the nation and get an acceptable, consistent, pizza. Although you can walk into another local wood-fired restaurant somewhere else in the nation and get an equally wonderful pizza, they won't be the same. Both of the wood-fired pizzas are going to be a hell of a lot better than Pizza Hut's pizza, but they aren't created the same way. In a local restaurant you don't know what to expect. At Pizza Hut, you know exactly what to expect.

If You're Taking the MEE

If you're in a Uniform Bar Exam jurisdiction and will be taking the Multistate Essay Exam, then the best materials to use are the Analyses that are created and released by the National Conference of Bar Examiners.

The NCBE has created an Analysis for each and every MEE question. It is quite literally the answer key for that essay question, provides a scoring rubric for bar graders to use when scoring applicant answers, and "address[es] all legal and factual issues the drafters intended to raise in the question[]."

The Analyses are comprehensive and will go into much more

detail than you will need to in your essay answer. Although you will not want to copy *every part* of the Analysis when you're copying model answers (you would skip the summary and case citations, for example), the additional information only increases your knowledge and understanding of the law as you read those additional parts.

Using the Analyses is even better than using the released student sample answers because the Analyses are perfect answers. They are the idealized answers that the creators of your test have envisioned applicants should submit. There is no better source for learning and perfecting how to write MEE answers.

For this reason, the MEE Analyses are what I have my own students use. They are the best.

You can get a few MEEs and Analyses for free from the NCBE website. The remaining ones which are not offered for free can be purchased there as well.

If You're Taking the Bar Exam in California or Another Non-UBE Jurisdiction

Those taking the MEE as part of the UBE are lucky to have such an amazing resource like the Analyses at their disposal. But when you're in another jurisdiction, like California or Florida, you have to find a way to make your options work. The question is, what do you use? Released student answers? Or commercial answers?

To the degree that consistency in essay answers helps your bar exam performance, commercial answers are preferable. On the other hand, to the degree that 20% of the law will be tested 80% of the time, and you should be practicing essays in the proportion in which they will be tested, using the last ten or more years of released sample answers is preferable.

With these two competing interests, which appear to conflict with each other, what should you do? Should you get released answers off a state bar website for free? Should you purchase a commercial essay answer book?

One option is to take this approach: Use commercial essay books for Stages 1 and 2. Make a concerted effort to find the testing frequency of your jurisdiction (a test frequency chart for both California and the UBE is available for free at FckTheBar.com, and adjust your use of the commercial materials so that you are generally adhering to the same testing frequency. When you advance to Stages 3 and 4, use the essay questions from the state bar websites. Go through them systematically, so you are getting proportionate practice.

By the time you are in Stages 3 and 4, you will have already benefitted from the consistency of the commercial book to learn how to write essay answers, and can now take advantage of experiencing the testing frequency that your jurisdiction likes to test. Remember Pareto's principle! This option is a bit of a bootstrap method to improve the results you might otherwise get by using only one of the essay sources.

If you're in California, there is another option. This option gives you commercially prepared answers which are consistent in structure, style, and rule statements, and which are available for every single essay question in the past ten years. You want to have all the reliability of consistent answers which help you to learn everything content-wise, along with the benefit of proportionate practice so that you are spending 80% of your time on the 20% of material that the bar examiners are sure to test you on. This combination gives incredible results and is what I use with my students.

FAILING ANSWERS

For the love of God, do NOT use failing answers for <u>any reason</u>. There are one hundred and one different ways to write a failing answer. You don't need to be an expert on any of them. You need to be an expert on writing a passing answer. What you focus on, you become. If you want high scores, pay attention to what gets high scores!

———

The Basic IRAC

I would be remiss if I overlooked a discussion of IRAC when talking about essay writing on the bar exam. You most assuredly already know what IRAC is from law school. On the off-chance that you don't, here's a quick little explanation. IRAC is an acronym that stands for Issue, Rule, Analysis, and Conclusion. It's the skeletal structure for legal writing. Each of these is a necessary part of performing a legal analysis, which is what you must do on law school exams as well as the bar exam.

As you copy sample answers, you will see that they use the IRAC format, and so should you. Some sample answers present the IRAC format in an overt way (think commercial essay answers). Others may use it in a more sophisticated manner where they weave the rule and analysis back and forth (think released essay answers).

The I: Issue

Spotting legal issues is the first part of thinking like a lawyer. Depending on the facts presented to you, you must be able to recognize facts that implicate legal issues. It signals to the grader that you can be given raw facts and know if there are legal implications. If you cannot spot a legal issue when it is presented, then you do not know the law very thoroughly or are not picking up on legal issues when they are presented in subtle or non-obvious ways. You demonstrate how much you know not just by what issues you include, but which ones you leave out.

The R: Rule

There are certain legal rules applicable to certain legal issues. Knowing which rule is applicable is how you demonstrate your proficiency in this area. This comes by being able to remember and state the rule on demand. You may also need to distinguish an applicable rule from another rule which may appear to be suitable, but for some reason isn't.

One of the biggest mistakes bar takers make is spending their time regurgitating rules of law. Although stating the appropriate rule of law is a critical element of writing a passing essay, don't fall into the trap of thinking more is better. Of course, you mean well - you want to show the bar grader how much law you know, and how hard you worked to prepare for the exam. Unfortunately, if you have thrown in the proverbial kitchen sink, then the bar grader is left to assume you can't distinguish between relevant legal rules upon which the case turns and irrelevant or less relevant rules.

The A: Analysis

The analysis is the "meat" of the entire exercise. This is where you show you understand the law and how to think like a lawyer by taking the facts presented and applying the legal rules to them. You demonstrate why that particular legal rule applies and how it applies to the instant fact pattern. If the legal rule is made up of elements, you must address each element in turn. If there are factors, you weigh each one. In going through this process, you bring the reader along for each step. Walk them through it, so they understand it. Show the math, as it were.

The analysis is a crucial part of writing a good essay, which very often leaves bar takers (especially repeaters) scratching their head. They wonder what in the world the bar graders are looking for. Often it seems as though it's shrouded in mystery, or that perhaps the difference between passing and failing is in the luck of the draw (i.e., which bar grader you get). Although grading essays is indeed subjective to some degree, there really is a pattern to writing good essay answers.

Have you ever wondered about those anecdotes repeaters tell about how they ran out of time and had to fly through their last essay, only to find out that that essay received their highest score? Or how they got the most points on the subject they knew the least about? That type of thing does happen, and it happens very often. Ever wonder why that is? It's because when law students have nothing else to rely on, they rely on their common sense and powers of reason. They use their brain to think of what the answer should be, and they write that. There's nothing else stored in their brain to write (or not enough time to get it all on paper), so they get right to the point and explain the thought process.

Do you know what that's called? It's called analysis. It is the ever-elusive A in IRAC. It is the single most challenging portion of legal writing that most bar takers face. For the most part, everyone accepted into law school already thinks in this manner, so it is taken for granted. It is natural for your mind to work quickly and make those leaps of analysis because you're so smart. However, when you make those leaps and skip right to the end (the conclusion), you have made the error of being conclusory. As you probably know by now, being conclusory is very bad and will cost you tons of points.

I recall when I first started "getting it." It had taken me longer than I expected to get the whole analysis thing. I kept being conclusory in my legal writing. I didn't understand what I was missing. Then I finally took a step back and made it really simple. Ridiculously simple. I pretended like I was in kindergarten. I kept it to one thought per sentence. *I stopped assuming the reader knew anything or could follow a premise to its logical conclusion. I started walking the reader through every little part of the thought process.* The result was that I became a better legal writer. I started analyzing. Once I "got it," it was like a lens was removed from my eyes. It all made sense, and it was never an issue again.

So if you feel like you're just not getting it, that it's too hard or you're not smart enough, relax. My money is on the probability that you are smart enough. In fact, you need to write as though you are *less intelligent.* Take a step back and simplify everything. Start stating all those unstated assumptions and logical deductions you are making in your mind, and you will find that your writing improves.

The analysis is the most important to the bar examiners, so it should be the most important to you, too. It is imperative that you learn how to do a strong analysis and lead the reader through the logical processes you take to reach your legal conclusion.

THE C: CONCLUSION

Finally, conclude your analysis by stating an outcome. Be authoritative and confident, avoiding equivocal language. But remain professional! Avoid using terminology which demeans anyone who comes to an alternative conclusion.

This is the least important part of the essay in the sense that you just need to reach a conclusion and have established your reasons for doing so. The conclusion should be brief; no more than one sentence is typically necessary.

9

SUBSTANTIVE REVIEW

Although this chapter is titled "Substantive Review," most of this chapter could have just as easily been placed in the long list of benefits that I wrote about earlier in the book. That's because as you will soon read, copying model answers provides almost all of the substantive review you will need over the course of bar prep. As such, I have continued the numbering sequence here.

BENEFIT #11: RE-LEARNING THE LAW THROUGH PRACTICE

Copying model answers should be an exercise in refreshing your recollection. You should have a frame of reference for the material that you see in the essays and answers. After all, you did go to law school for three years.

When you read through fact patterns and copy the model answers which provide the rule of law, and you see a legal analysis in action, all your knowledge in that area will come flooding back to the forefront of your mind. You may have stopped thinking about Torts after you took that exam your 1L year, but the knowledge is there.

Your ability to understand and work with the concepts is there. You simply need to recall it. The process of copying model answers is more than sufficient to activate those memory banks and get your brain right back to where it was when you were taking Torts.

This is why you do not need to listen to or sit through lectures or read outlines! It is a much less efficient use of your time because all the necessary information is automatically going to be re-ignited as you do essays. Not to mention you just spent three years going to lectures, reading case law, and writing outlines.

If you aren't ready to walk into the bar exam the day after law school graduation, then what makes you think that doing *more* of that will prepare you for the bar exam? What gets you ready to take the bar exam is practicing the bar exam tasks.

If you are a repeater, a substantive review is that much more unnecessary. Unless you failed the bar because you simply didn't prepare at all, you would have undoubtedly already gone through all the material within the last six months. So if you've done a traditional bar prep, you probably went through the material (lectures, outlines, mnemonics, flashcards, worksheets, etc.) at length.

In fact, there's a good chance that it was *because* you spent so much time doing substantive review instead of taking practice exams, that you scored below what you are capable of. So in this scenario, more than the others, no substantive review is necessary. Improved skill on the bar exam tasks is what is in order.

BENEFIT #12: LEARNING THE LAW THROUGH PRACTICE

Sometimes you will face bar exam material that you either never learned in law school or you just don't "get." When you have no touchstone for legal principles, I recommend copying model answers just the same. At least at first. Although it is very difficult to do, do not worry about what you do and don't know when you're first getting started. Copy some model answers, see what legal rules the models provide, see how those rules apply in their analysis, and then gauge your understanding from there.

This does three things:

First, doing a few essays will give you some frame of reference for fact patterns in which this area of law is triggered. You will see what types of scenarios might be used in a test question or real life. Then when you read an outline later to learn this legal concept, you will have the ability to take the theoretical legal concepts in an outline and understand how they apply in a practical, real-world example. This will help you learn the concepts faster and more thoroughly.

Second, doing a few essays will give you a frame of reference for what the important and commonly tested issues are. Then when you read an outline later, you will know what concepts to zero in on and look at closely. You will also know what material you can speed through because it is unlikely to be tested. Spending a proportionate amount of time learning important concepts is much more effective and efficient. It's the 80/20 rule showing up again!

Third, doing a few essays might teach you the law! Remember back to your childhood when you were a young reader. Do you recall how new vocabulary words would pop up in books all the time? Words that if your teacher had written on the chalkboard in isolation, you wouldn't have had the foggiest idea of their meaning? Even with no knowledge of their definitions, you often learned the meaning of these words by their context in the book. You kind of got the gist of it by merely having read the sentences before it and the sentences after it. Your brain is so smart that it was able to deduce what that strange new word meant.

Of course, you weren't always right. Sometimes you were close, but not right on the money. But overall, your ability to deductively reason and take cues from context caused you to be able to learn a lot of vocabulary in a way that almost seemed like osmosis. Your brain still works that way. You will be surprised how much you "get" when you copy model answers and see the fact pattern, legal rule, and analysis all laid out for you.

If you think back, you might remember this happening in law school even. There was probably at least one legal concept that you didn't quite grasp when the professor was defining it for you in theory. However, once he described a situation in which it would apply, or once you read a case wherein the court analyzed the rule, it all made sense. That's the power of context.

WHEN IT'S TRULY NECESSARY TO SUPPLEMENT

If you have copied dozens of model answers and know that you're still in the dark on something, then you should go ahead and supplement with some other resources like a lecture or outline. You will know if this is necessary. When you understand something, you know it. When you're not sure, it feels rather iffy.

It's like when you see someone at the grocery store that you *think* looks like Jimmy from your Crossfit box, but you can't be quite sure. You awkwardly walk up to him only to realize it's not Jimmy at all! If that's the feeling you're getting about a legal principle, then go through that particular material in a supplemental fashion, but make quick work of it. There aren't any legal concepts that you shouldn't be able to get through in a half hour, or perhaps an hour if it's a real struggle for you. Once you've done that, get right back to practicing. Do not get sucked into the trap of thinking you don't know it well enough and need to memorize the law.

You DO NOT need to have anything memorized before you practice! This is the ass-backward way of doing things! You solidify the material in your brain AS you practice. If you want the content to easily flow out of your brain, through your fingers, and into your laptop on exam day, then start practicing before you feel ready! Do not delay. S t r u g g l e through the material. The struggle brings the growth.

For this reason, I do not advocate reading any outlines or listening to any lectures or adding anything supplemental into your bar prep at the beginning. You need to start doing because you will find that all that supplemental shit is probably not needed at all (or very, very little is necessary).

You'll also better avoid getting stuck in that limbo stage where people think they need to review "just a little bit more," and then they never get to actual practice. So do not add supplemental material until you're *at least* one third through bar prep, preferably halfway. There will still be plenty of time at the halfway mark. So if you can resist until that point, you will be in a much stronger position than you would have been otherwise.

Today: June 3 (52 days until July 25)

52 days = 7.429 weeks

1/3 of 7.429 weeks = 17.334 days

1/2 of 7.429 weeks = 26.001 days

10

PERFORMANCE TESTS

Along with the essays, the performance test (PT) makes up the written portion of the bar exam. The total weight of the written portion depends on your jurisdiction. In California and on the UBE, the written portion is worth 50%. The performance test portion specifically is worth ~14% of your total score in California (based on one PT). On the UBE, it's worth 20% (divided between two MPTs).

This makes the performance test worth more than an essay answer, meaning that you want to be proficient at this task as well as the others to get those points needed to get you beyond a passing score! The performance test is not only worth more than an essay, but it is also longer than an essay, taking up ninety minutes of your time for a single performance test.

The performance test is a closed universe test, meaning that all the information you need to know is presented to you in the materials. No outside legal knowledge is necessary, and you don't need to regurgitate any memorized material.

Essentially what is being tested is your ability to think like a lawyer and present a cogent piece of work product. The test is designed to simulate a real-world assignment like one you might face in the practice of law. For the UBE, this often comes in the form of a persuasive brief or an objective memo that you are drafting for a managing partner. In California, your task might be to prepare a closing argument or a contract. The type of tasks that might be tested varies.

The performance test is presented in two batches of documents: a File and a Library. The File contains all the real-world documents that are related to the task. Think of them as the fact pattern: letters, emails, transcripts, contracts... any of these types of things might be contained in the file. It's as if someone walked into your law office and presented you with a legal problem.

The Library contains all the legal authority that is related to the task. Think of it as the legal research you'd have after spending a day in the law library looking up the law on the fact pattern that has been presented to you.

Between the File and the Library, you have been presented with the raw materials that lawyers use every day to do their job. Now you have to show you are up to the task.

The way you prepare for this portion of the exam is the same way you prepare for the essays - you practice taking performance tests, you learn the format of a well-written answer, and you get good at organizing and writing answers. You will need to demonstrate the following skills:

- Can you follow directions?

- Can you perform the task required in the set amount of time?

- Do you know how to judge the importance of smaller tasks within the large task and apportion them the appropriate amount of time?

- Can you quickly get through a large amount of material,

all while judging which information is essential, which is unimportant, which is reliable, and which is missing?

- Can you extract the legal rules and principles from case, statutory, and other law?

- Do you know which legal authorities have more weight than others?

- Do you know which legal rules are no longer "good law"?

- Can you recognize an actual or potential ethical or professional violation? Do you know how to handle it properly when you do?

- Can you use common sense to recognize or anticipate problems?

- Are you able to think of feasible solutions and formulate a plan?

- Can you communicate all of the above, whether it be to a judge, a boss, a client, a jury, opposing counsel, or someone else?

- Is the communication effective? That is, is it well thought out, well developed, organized, persuasive, and professional?

Think of the performance test as a work assignment. Assume you have passed the bar and are working in your first job as a practicing attorney. Your boss drops this assignment on your desk at 3:30 pm with a note that it *has to* go out by the close of business. That's exactly how you should be thinking of the performance test.

Obviously, you will have all your legal knowledge from law

school, but more importantly than that, your boss hired you because you have a good head on your shoulders, are professional, think like the well-trained lawyer that you are, and even have common sense to boot. Moreover, since you're an ambitious first-year associate, you want to impress your boss with a stellar product (not to mention avoid malpractice by getting the legal analysis wrong).

Practicing the performance test will take the same form as practicing the essays. You are going to read through a performance test packet (the File and the Library), and then, depending on what stage you're in, you're going to write out a complete answer.

- In Stage 1, you will simply copy the model answer.

- In Stage 2, you will copy the model answer, then write your own answer immediately after.

- In Stage 3, you will write your own answer before looking at the model answer, and then copy the model.

- In Stage 4, you will write your own answer. You are free to skim over the model answer to make sure you didn't make any fatal errors.

As you copy model answers, just like the essays, you will want to make mental notes of the differences between your answer and the model answer. See what the model answer did better than you that you can learn from and emulate.

When you first start writing out your own answers, don't worry too much about the clock. You will likely not finish in the ninety minutes allotted. In this earlier stage (Stage 2), you want to learn how to write an adequate and complete answer, not an exhaustive one.

At this point, you should be figuring out the best way to approach the performance test.

- Do you like to read the file or library first?

- Do you like to make notes on scratch paper, or directly onto the computer?

- Do you like to highlight the material, with each color having its own meaning?

- Do you like to underline?

- Do you like to tear apart the booklets, or keep them intact?

- Do you like to start writing right away, or do you have to have all the sections organized and planned before you write your first complete sentence?

- Do you spend too much time reading the file and library, or do you spend too little time and miss critical information?

Work out all these kinks at this early stage, so you find an approach and rhythm that works for you. That way you have a system you can immediately implement when you do a performance test and waste not a precious minute of your time.

As you continue to practice, you will start holding yourself accountable to the time limit (Stages 3 & 4). Each performance test contains a lot of material, and you can get lost by spending too much time in one area or going into too much detail. You have to get your pacing down and make sure you finish in time. Completing the required task is an essential part of scoring well. So at this point, you have to stick to ninety minutes.

The final stage of performance test practice is making sure the content of your answer is good, each and every time. This includes the overall organization of the answer, extrapolating the legal rules and principles accurately, performing proper fact analysis, writing good fact statements, etc. Your content should get better and better with each performance test you practice, just as it does with the essays.

Realize that as you progress in your essay practice, those writing skills you're learning are going to be translating to your performance test answers, as well. Nevertheless, don't go easy on yourself when evaluating your answer compared to the model. You may know what you meant, but the grader doesn't. If it's not clearly spelled out in your answer, you will get no points. So evaluate your answer at its face value.

If feasible, get yourself a performance test buddy at Stage 4. You can take a timed test together, then read each other's answers. Be committed to giving helpful critiques. Don't be defensive in response to the critique. Remember that you aren't in law school anymore - your friends are no longer your competition! The bar exam isn't a zero-sum game. You can both pass without it detracting from the other person. So be helpful and give honest and useful feedback.

WHERE TO GET PRACTICE PERFORMANCE TESTS

When practicing the performance test you need to work from a hardcopy. You can download and print past CA performance tests and Multistate Performance Tests for free from a variety of places. Links can be found at FckTheBar.com.

When choosing which performance tests (which tasks) to practice, there are three approaches.

The first approach is to simply take the most recent performance tests administered. Let's say you are going to do twelve practice performance tests. Just look up the last twelve and do those. The primary benefit to this option is that you will be the most familiar with how the examiners are currently testing in the performance test.

The second approach is to browse through the past exams and choose as good of a mixture of tasks as you can find. The obvious benefit of this option is that you will ensure having practiced a wide variety of tasks. There's one caveat to this: the bar examiners do not test each type of task with equal frequency. Therefore, you may have done the required task before, but perhaps only once.

If you look at the frequency of past exams, you will see that the bar examiners seem to assign specific types of tasks, such as persuasive briefs and objective memos more frequently than other tasks. If you don't practice according to the relative frequency with which the tasks are tested, you could be doing yourself a disservice.

The third approach, and perhaps the safest, is to split the difference between the two other approaches. Choose half of your performance tests based on the most recent administrations and the other half based on a cross-section of the different types of tasks that pop up from time to time. This will put you on-trend with the latest exams while ensuring your practice is well-rounded.

THE PERFORMANCE TEST TRACKER

Use the FTB Performance Test Tracker to keep track of your progress. You can see which performance tests you have completed, as well as what types of tasks you have practiced. Simply fill in the information after each performance test you take. You can download it at FckTheBar.com.

WHAT YOU ABSOLUTELY NEED TO KNOW ABOUT THE PERFORMANCE TEST

While there are quite a few things about the performance test that are not set in stone (such as whether you read the File or Library first), a few things are non-negotiable. Here they are:

- NEVER use your real name. Anytime your name would be appropriate (which is pretty much only in a Memorandum heading, or at the end of a letter or court filing), write "Examinee" or "Applicant."

- ALWAYS read the Memorandum first. The Memorandum to "Examinee" or "Applicant" is your instructions. This is where you are given your task. Regardless of whether you read the File or Library first, this is where to start.

- Don't waste time trying to create bluebook citations. Whenever you need to cite legal authority, the case name, year, and court is sufficient. You could even leave the year out. For example: "In *Jones v. Smith*, the Supreme Court decided that..." Subsequent citations can be truncated down to *Jones*, so long as the short form is unambiguous. Likewise, for statutes, write: "Under the Smith Act, enacted by State Legislature in 1990, felons must..."

- Don't waste time trying to format your document to match the example document. You get absolutely no points for doing so, and the formatting will most likely be distorted during printing, anyway. If you wish, you may simply write "[On Letterhead]", "[On Pleading Paper]", or whichever format is appropriate, at the very top of your document.

- Always be professional! Even if your task is to write a memorandum to your supervising attorney, always state it professionally. It reflects poorly on you to say that opposing counsel is an idiot and has no chance of winning because they have no witnesses. The bar examiners are looking to see if you treat yourself and others within the legal community with respect. Therefore, there is no place for name-calling, profanity, sarcasm, or the like. Be sincere and professional.

- If there appears to be an ethical issue present, such as a potential conflict of interest, but it is not an obvious part of the task, make sure you address it appropriately. Let's say you have been given the task of drafting a client letter for your boss. The letter is about the client's likelihood of prevailing on a breach of contract claim. After reading through the File, you find out that one of the firm's partners is a stockholder in the opposing party's company, and this information wasn't available before now. What you do is draft the letter as assigned, but in an appropriate place in the letter, write a note concerning the conflict in brackets. For example:

> *While reviewing the file, I came across a small note indicating that Partner is a stockholder in the opposing party's company. As such, Partner would personally stand to lose money if our client prevailed on his breach of conflict claim. Even if our client did not prevail, the litigation costs would affect the company's profitability, thereby still affecting Partner's personal financial interests. It appears that this information wasn't known when the firm ran its usual conflict check. Please advise whether we should continue working on this case.*

Your "boss," who will be reviewing the letter before it is sent, will become apprised of the ethical issue and determine what should be done. Meanwhile, you have shown the grader that you can recognize a potential ethical issue when it arises, and know how to address it appropriately. Remember, you must always have your ethics "hat" on.

- When writing a persuasive piece, do not omit rebuttals to arguments which opposing counsel is likely to make. In real life, opposing counsel answers your complaint, and then you get a chance to reply to their answer. On the performance test, you don't get to wait for opposing counsel to make their arguments, so you must anticipate what they will be, where appropriate. For the sake of the

performance test, the arguments you should anticipate are
only the obvious/major ones. Don't start arguing on behalf of
opposing counsel, saying they will argue this, that, and the
other thing. If it is warranted (and it will be clear to you if
it is), just rebut the strongest argument or two that
opposing counsel will make.

- If you must draft a statement of facts for a persuasive
  assignment, be careful that your use of facts does not
  become deceptive. This goes for using legal authority
  persuasively, as well. You never want to put your candor
  into question by spinning facts or legal precedent, or by
  omitting germane information.

PERFORMANCE TEST TIPS & TRICKS

In addition to those things which you absolutely need to know about
the performance test, there are a bunch which isn't necessary, but
helpful nonetheless. Try out these tips and tricks:

1. GIVE YOURSELF AN EXTRA TEN MINUTES

When practicing, always set your timer for eighty minutes. Get
used to finishing with ten minutes to spare. Then on the actual exam,
set the alarm provided in the software to also go off after eighty
minutes. (Make sure to practice using the software and its alarm func-
tion ahead of time.) With a "bonus" of ten minutes, there are few
problems you can't fix - whether you didn't get the last section done,
need to make some revisions, or just want to re-read and edit for
errors, you now have the time to do so.

2. KEEP THE MEMORANDUM IN FRONT OF YOU AT ALL TIMES

When time starts, the first thing you should do is find the Memorandum to Applicant/Examinee (at the beginning of the File). Tear it

out, read it, highlight and make any notes necessary, read it again, then keep it in front of you for the remainder of the test. It is a good idea to employ the use of a book stand during the performance test, so you can keep the Memorandum easily accessible, and out the pile of papers you will inevitably have in front of you (especially if you like to take the File and Library apart). Don't waste precious time trying to find that Memorandum when you need to remember specific instructions.

Additionally, make sure you periodically re-read the instructions. There are times when the instructions will seem general at first, but as you dig deeper into the assignment and become more familiar with the contents of the File and Library, you will find that the instructions are more narrow and help you to define your scope a little bit. So you always want to ensure you're not veering off course or exceeding the scope of the call. If you're lucky, the Memorandum will even provide the entire organization and headings for your document. It is a very important sheet of paper!

3. READ THE FILE FIRST

After you have read the Memorandum (which should ALWAYS come first), read the File. In real life, you do not perform legal research until you have a case and a set of facts because you don't know what will be relevant. It just makes sense then that you read the File first, so you have something to hang your hat on, as it were.

4. DO A QUICK READ THROUGH, THEN RE-READ FOR CONTENT

Even though you should read the File first, do it very quickly. Then read through the Library quickly, as well. Your time will be much better spent once you have a brief overview of what you are dealing with. Don't get caught up with trying to catch all the details contained in the File, or all the legal rules in the Library.

Once you've done a quick read, you will know if you should then go back to the File to gather facts, or if you should dig into the

Library and get your rules. The first, fast read is simply to get the flavor of the assignment and to give you enough information so you can best direct your attention going forward.

5. Employ A Shorthand Technique For Quick Reference

When drafting your outline and taking notes, you need a quick and easy way to be able to refer to facts in the File, or law from the Library. You do not want to waste time writing everything out long-hand, or flipping around trying to find the source of that information later so you can quote it. Use this technique:

> The File is where the Facts are found.
> F = File = Facts

> The Library is where the Law is found.
> L = Library = Law

The pages in both the F and L are pre-numbered. This makes page 10 of the file = F 10; page 4 of the library = L 4

Each page is broken up into paragraphs. The first whole paragraph found on a page is paragraph 1, the second paragraph is paragraph 2, and so on. If the first paragraph on the page is an incomplete paragraph (a continuation of the paragraph from the previous page), then that is paragraph 0.

Therefore, paragraph 2 on page 10 of the file = F 10/2; paragraph 0 on page 4 of the library = L 4/0.

Using this technique, you can quickly make a note of where you found certain information. When creating your outline or making notes, all you need to do is write a few key words about the information, then write the reference. For example:

P purchased car 1/1/90 (F 10/2)
Elements of grand theft (L 4/0)

This will save you tons of time as you can fully list all the facts and legal authority you need to in a short amount of time. Then when you are ready to write your answer, you can instantly go directly to the paragraph containing the information you are seeking.

If you want to be even more specific, you can choose to number the lines on each page and cite to the line number as opposed to the paragraph number. It will give you an even more specific reference, but may not be time-efficient since you will then spend time numbering the lines. This is a strategy for when your File contains a transcript which will have pre-numbered lines.

6. USE COLORED HIGHLIGHTERS

If you organize best using colors and visual cues, trying using different colored highlighters. Suppose your performance test is broken up into four major parts - maybe four causes of action (COA). Assign each one a different color. When you find legal rules in the Library related to one COA, use the assigned color to highlight that law. When you find facts supporting that same COA, use the same color to highlight those facts. Do this for each COA. As you work on each section, just look for that color in the File and Library and ignore everything else. This helps you focus on the relevant information and not get distracted by the rest.

7. NEVER LOOK LIKE YOU RAN OUT OF TIME

After you've organized and planned your answer, you're ready to begin writing. First, write down all your sections and their headers. Then go ahead and write out the first section or two (make sure you have a strong start to impress the graders). Then, skip to the end! Yep, you read that right - skip all the middle sections and write your last section.

Now, no matter what happens, you won't have a weak finish. Graders look to see if you ran out of time, and a weak finish will affect you poorly. With this strategy you are utilizing the effects of primacy and recency to your greatest benefit.

If you think that you can't do the last section because you haven't done the previous ones, you would be wrong in almost every situation. The last section on the performance test would rarely be wholly dependent on the legal conclusion reached in the prior sections. Plus, performance tests are designed so that once you have the organization correct, each section is pretty much an independent analysis. [Note: If the last section is a sub-section of a greater issue, you can't just do the last sub-section. In that case, you must do the entire last section with all its sub-sections.]

After you've written the last section, go back and finish the middle sections in their respective order. If you run out of time, it will be hidden somewhere in a middle section, and not as evident to the graders. This will minimize the overall effect of running out of time on your score.

A final tip to help even more is to write out the rule for each section when you write down the section headers. Deciphering what the legal standard is for each issue, and articulating that rule well, can be a significant part of your performance test (and usually where much time is spent). If you do this part now, you will already have the I and R for the entire performance test. Then you write the first 1 or 2 sections, then the last section.

If you're running out of time towards the end, it is much easier to breeze through an analysis and conclusion. You don't want to be racing the clock and trying to formulate the legal rule - you are too stressed in that situation for your brain to think efficiently and your rule statement won't be as good as it would be if you had thought it out well.

11

MBE PRACTICE

The Multistate Bar Exam, or "MBE" for short, is a 200 question multiple-choice test created by the National Conference of Bar Examiners (NCBE). Every state (except Louisiana) administers the MBE as part of their bar exam. The MBE tests Civil Procedure, Constitutional Law, Contracts, Criminal Law and Procedure, Evidence, Real Property, and Torts.

Although the MBE consists of 200 questions, only 175 are scored. The remaining 25 "pretest questions," are included by the NCBE to test new questions. The highest possible MBE score is 175 "raw." Raw scores are then "scaled," so that scores are consistent from exam to exam. In this way, examinees don't benefit from taking an "easier" MBE, nor are they penalized if they get a "harder" MBE.

The scaled score is used when calculating your overall score by whichever jurisdiction you are testing in. Check your jurisdiction to find out what weight they give the MBE in their overall scoring rubric. If your jurisdiction administers the Uniform Bar Exam (UBE), the MBE counts as 50% of your score.

The MBE is a multiple-choice test. Each MBE question contains a fact pattern, followed by a question (the call), then four answer choices. The correct answer is the "best" answer. You do not lose points for choosing an incorrect answer, so if you cannot decide which answer option is the best, then it is better to guess than leave it blank. By guessing you have a 25% chance of getting the correct answer. If you have been able to eliminate one or two options as clearly incorrect, your chances go up. Blank answers, as well as multiple answers, are scored as incorrect.

NOT ALL MBEs ARE CREATED EQUAL

When I was studying for the bar exam, I thought all MBE questions were MBE questions. In other words, they're all the same. So the focus became: where can I get the most MBEs for the least amount of money? Like everyone else, I was trying to get the best bang for the buck and the most MBE practice possible.

Those of you who have taken the bar exam before will undoubtedly have heard some of your comrades walk out of MBE commenting, "That was so much harder than I expected it to be." Or perhaps you were the one feeling that way. In contrast, others will have walked out with the comment, "You thought it was harder? It didn't seem any worse than the practice questions I did."

There's a reason for this discrepancy. It turns out, not all MBE questions are authentic MBE questions. They are not all the same. Remember how I said that the MBE is created by the NCBE? The NCBE creates the MBE questions you will have on the actual MBE during the bar exam. They also release retired MBE questions to the public for practice purposes. Here's what the NCBE says about MBE questions:

 MBE questions are developed by drafting committees composed of recognized experts in the various subject areas. Before a test question is selected for inclusion in the MBE, it undergoes a multistage review process over the course of several years. Besides intensive review by the drafting committee members and testing specialists, each test question is reviewed by other national and state experts. All test questions must successfully pass all reviews before they are included in the MBE. After an MBE is administered, the performance of each test question is reviewed and evaluated by content and testing experts. This final review is conducted to ensure that the exam is graded fairly, particularly with regard to any questions affected by recent changes in the law.

Clearly, the NCBE creates and releases MBEs only after a rigorous process. If you want to practice with authentic MBEs that are going to allow you to ideally simulate and prepare for the real MBE, then you need to get your hands on these MBEs.

Unfortunately for bar examinees across the country, many bar prep companies, MBE books, and MBE test prep companies provide fake and/or outdated MBEs to their students. Examinees who rely on these materials to practice and prepare for their bar exam have been done a huge disservice, all in the name of turning a profit.

In order to publish or distribute authentic MBEs, which is copyrighted material, a license from the NCBE is required. The license costs money, in addition to royalties that must be paid each and every time a student purchases or uses the material. This significantly cuts into profits!

To make more money, companies create their own MBEs (read: fake). They won't call them fake. They'll call them "simulated questions," or some other more palatable name. Since fake MBEs are the property of the company/person who created them, and not the NCBE, no license is required, and no fees or royalties must be paid. The company can keep the money they get from you, and you're just left to taking your chances with their materials.

Another tactic they use is to provide outdated questions. The NCBE has been releasing retired, authentic questions for decades. Many of these questions were used on the bar exam in 1972. 1972!! They're almost 50 years old! Would you drive a 45-year-old car cross-country? Are you trusting 45-year-old MBE questions to pass the bar?

The NCBE even provides some of these very old questions for

free on its website. However, the NCBE instructs students NOT TO USE THEM! Here's what the NCBE says about these questions:

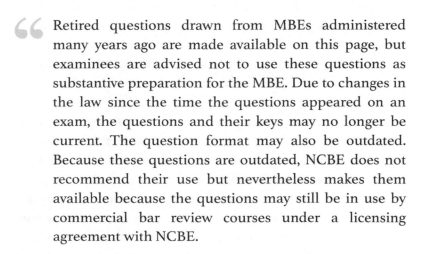

> Retired questions drawn from MBEs administered many years ago are made available on this page, but examinees are advised not to use these questions as substantive preparation for the MBE. Due to changes in the law since the time the questions appeared on an exam, the questions and their keys may no longer be current. The question format may also be outdated. Because these questions are outdated, NCBE does not recommend their use but nevertheless makes them available because the questions may still be in use by commercial bar review courses under a licensing agreement with NCBE.

The reason a company will use outdated questions is because even though they still have to pay a licensing and royalty fee, the fee for the very old questions is nominal. It costs very, very little. The royalty fee for the updated and reliable MBEs comes at a premium. If a company uses outdated questions, they can add hundreds and hundreds of questions for a shockingly low cost to them. They can also claim to be using authentic, NCBE licensed questions (because they are). What they won't tell you is that they're providing questions that the NCBE itself warns examinees NOT to use.

As of this writing, there are exactly 620 authentic, real, and updated MBE questions released by the NCBE, which are current and reliable for use as practice. That's it. Believe it or not, 620 questions is all you need to prepare for the MBE. I'll show you how to use them. If you're using a company that provides more than 620 questions, you can bet your bottom dollar that you're getting a mixed bag of fake and/or outdated questions.

How will you know whether you're getting authentic questions? Or if they're outdated questions? Simple. Go to the copyright page of the book. If the questions are real, there will be a copyright for the

National Conference of Bar Examiners, and the copyright year will be listed.

Look closely though! Some books use a *mix* of real and fake questions, so there will be a copyright included, but only *some* of the questions are real. Or there will be a mix of old and new questions. If you're using an online provider of MBE questions, dig around the website and/or email them to find out where their questions come from.

If you are insistent on getting more than those 620 authentic, real, and updated MBE questions, you don't need to pay for them. You can find an additional 1,212 released questions for free by going directly to the NCBE's website, or by getting the freebies available on FckThe-Bar.com.

With my students, I only use the 620 authentic and current MBEs that come straight from the NCBE because if it's not what *I* would use for *myself* if it were *MY bar card* on the line, then I wouldn't even consider passing it off to my students.

Endurance is Key

You will need to incorporate some endurance training into your MBE study plan. On most regular days you will do a smaller number of MBEs, like twenty to thirty. However, on these special days, you will scrap the regular plan and do MBEs endurance style. For those of you who will be taking the bar for the first time, you do not yet understand the level of pure mental exhaustion that you will have on MBE day.

Your brain will feel like jello after the MBE. You don't want it to feel like jello *during* the MBE. The other portions of the bar exam do not come close to using the same amount of mental effort and concentration that the MBE requires. You will probably feel exhausted and drained after the first session. It is difficult to return from the lunch break and know you have to do it all over again. I guarantee you will hit the wall at least once during MBE day. Doing 200 MBEs in six hours is a world apart from doing twenty or thirty

MBEs per day. Therefore, you need to practice doing large numbers of MBEs to build your endurance and prepare yourself for the enormous challenge you will face on day two of the bar exam.

I recommend doing one full-length mock MBE approximately two-thirds to three-quarters through your bar preparation period where you tackle an entire 200 questions in one six-hour day (but make sure to give yourself at least an hour lunch break in between sessions). Don't grade your practice exam that day; you will be too exhausted. Eat a good dinner, watch a brainless comedy, and get a good night's sleep. When you wake up refreshed the following day, you can grade the exam and spend the rest of the day doing a review of your answers.

Ideally, you might also set aside two other days on your calendar to do a half-length practice exam of 100 questions. It is recommended to incorporate these approximately one-quarter and half-way through your bar preparation period.

On these days, do the questions in the morning, then grade and review the exam for the rest of the day. If your brain is feeling too fried from the MBEs to do the review immediately, then do the review the next day, and switch to a different study task for the remainder of the day.

1/4 through prep: 100 question endurance session

1/2 through prep: 100 question endurance session

3/4 through prep: 200 question endurance session

PICK YOUR NUMBER

The next order of business is determining what number of MBEs you need to do each and every day. The number of MBEs you want to accomplish over the course of your bar prep is up to you. However, I would caution you not to go below 1,200. As for the higher range, more than 2,000 is likely unnecessary and will offer diminishing returns. So long as you are using real, authentic, and current MBEs, and practicing properly, somewhere between 1,200 and 2,000 is sufficient.

Once you have figured out how many practice questions you want to do, you need to break it down into a daily pace so you know how many you must do daily to meet your goal. Let's go through two scenarios to give you an idea of how this might work out for you.

Let's presume you want to be cautious in your preparations, so you wish to practice 2,000 MBEs by exam day. The first thing you need to do is determine how long you have to study. Let's say you have ten weeks, and you are going to do MBEs Monday through Saturday.

- 10 weeks x 6 days = 60 MBE days

Over the course of your full-length practice exam and two half-length exams, you will have knocked out 400 MBEs and 4 days, which leaves you with:

- 60 MBE days - 4 endurance MBE practice days = 56 days
- 2,000 MBEs - 400 MBEs = 1,600 MBEs

Therefore, over the course of the remaining 56 MBE days you will need to do 1,600 MBEs.

- 1,600 MBEs / 56 days = 28 MBEs per day

In summary, you would plan to practice MBEs Monday through Saturday for the ten weeks leading up to the exam. Each day you practice twenty-eight MBEs. In addition to that, you will designate four special days to get some endurance training. One day will be a full-length practice exam of 200 questions. The following day is a review. The two other days will be half-length practice exams of 100 questions each and review in the afternoon.

Some of you may be in a different boat. Let's say you are doing the quick and dirty version of prep. You have six weeks and are shooting to practice 1,200 MBEs by test day. With limited time, you'll need to cut down your endurance practice to only one full-length day. (Never,

ever, ever, skip doing a full-length practice MBE exam!) This would be your equation:

- 6 weeks x 6 days = 36 MBE days
- 36 MBE days - 1 full length MBE (2 days) = 34 MBE days
- 1,200 MBEs - 1 full length MBE (200 questions) = 1,000 MBEs
- 1,000 MBEs / 34 days = 29 MBEs per day

Once you have figured out how many MBEs you need to do on a daily basis in order to meet your goal and be prepared by test day, it is critical that you DO THEM each and every day. Studying for the MBE is not complex. Although you must know complexities of the law in order to score well on the MBE, the study approach is fairly straightforward. In the end, to become the best at MBEs that you can, you need to practice, practice, practice. You must implement the plan to make it work.

Make daily MBE practice a habit right from the start. If you hate MBEs, do them as your first study task of the day so you can get them over with and move on to essays. You will not have them hanging over your head the rest of the day, and you will feel a great deal of accomplishment by getting them taken care of first. If you like MBEs better than essays, end with them as your incentive for getting through the essays, or perhaps do them mid-day as a way to break up your day.

Whenever you choose to do them, make it a daily habit so that you don't miss a day. What starts as a single missed day turns into two, which turns into a week. A week of missed MBEs is almost a whole exam, which is difficult to make up.

As you will find out a little later in the book, I suggest doing twenty to thirty MBEs for every 4-hour Study Block. If you're studying full-time and can complete two blocks in a day, then you would do forty to sixty MBEs per day.

Good Form

When practicing MBE questions, it is crucial that you do them the correct way to get the most benefit. The goal is not to do twenty-five MBEs just to check that off your daily to-do list. The goal is to test your knowledge, fill in any gaps, and improve your competency so that your score improves. As with physical exercise, where you get better results if you use proper form, it is the same with MBE practice.

1. Wait until you have finished all your MBE questions before looking up any answers.

I know it is tempting to look up the answer to a question when you have spent time agonizing over what answer could be the "correct" one (i.e., the "best" answer). The need for instant gratification has no place on the MBE. There are many reasons why:

- It breaks up your concentration, thus diminishing your mental stamina and discipline.

- You won't get the same satisfaction on the actual MBE.

- It can build a false sense of security when you get an answer correct; in the alternative, it can shake your confidence when you get a question (or a few questions in a row) wrong.

- Looking up the answer gives you the benefit of reading rules of law mid-test, which you won't have the luxury of doing on the real thing.

- It is an inefficient use of time, resulting from flipping back and forth between answering questions and looking up answers.

2. But don't wait too long.

An essential aspect of MBE practice is doing a good, proper review of each question. You want to leave enough time to not only do practice questions but to review the answers fully, as well. If you break up the practice MBEs from the review of those questions for too long, you will waste time. You'd be surprised how quickly your mind forgets the questions you just answered, and you will have to re-read the question just to review the answer. Worse yet, you will probably have forgotten what you were thinking when you chose the answer you did.

You want to have the question still fresh in your mind, along with both the answer option you chose (and why you chose it) and the answer options you did not choose (and why you didn't choose them). Therefore, make sure you review the answers as soon as you're finished doing all the questions. Don't put it off until later in the day.

3. Read all the answer explanations when it is time to look up the answers.

The only exception for this rule is when you chose the correct answer and you are absolutely sure why that answer was correct. Also, you can skip over the answer explanations for incorrect answer options (that you were correct in not choosing) so long as you are absolutely sure why that answer option was incorrect. For all other scenarios, read the answer explanation!

4. Articulate the operant rule of law.

When going over the answer explanations, try to articulate the applicable rule of law in your mind before reading the answer explanation. For example, if the question turned on the mailbox rule, don't say to yourself, "A is correct because the letter was posted on July 1st." Think through the rule as if you were going to write it down in an essay. Say to yourself, "According to the mailbox rule, an offer is accepted when acceptance is posted to the offeror, not when it is received."

Each time you make an effort to do this, you solidify your knowledge of the law, which is going to better prepare you for the exam. Furthermore, sometimes, you don't realize that you are unable to articulate the rule of law until you try to do so.

When taking an objective test like the MBE, the answers are right in front of you. This can lead to a false sense of your abilities because you don't have to come up with the correct answer, you just have to pick it out of a lineup of options. Making yourself articulate the rule will help you find those gaps and fill them in. If you can't articulate the rule before you read the answer explanation, do so afterward to solidify what you just read.

SUBJECT ROTATION

When you're first starting prep, I advocate doing MBE practice subject by subject. For example, one day do Contracts MBEs (on the day you're doing Contracts essays). The next day, do Evidence MBEs (on the day you're doing Evidence essays). It is recommended that you do single-subject MBE practice for only the first third of bar prep, and do the remaining two-thirds with mixed-subject practice. This is how I coach my students. Focusing on single-subject practice in the beginning helps you dig into one subject per day, and your brain is getting flooded with all things Torts, or all things Evidence, etc. It diminishes the jumping around your brain will have to do and is more effective for solidifying that subject matter.

Later on during bar prep, after you've gone through all the subjects and given some individual attention to them, start doing mixed subject practice and continue on that way until the end of bar prep. You will be training your brain to be nimble and jump around from subject to subject, which is exactly what it will have to do on the bar exam, which is how the real MBE presents questions.

It takes more mental effort to switch between legal rules each time you move on to another question. Part of that challenge is simply determining as quickly as possible which subject area is being tested in the instant question. This is a much less efficient way of answering questions, but it is the way that it is done on the real MBE, so all the better to get familiar with it now.

You will need a way to keep track of your progress. Trackers will tell you what MBE subjects are your strongest and weakest because you will be tracking your scores after every practice session. Online MBE sites typically provide metrics for you. If you like to use hard-copy materials, then you can track your own metrics by using the FTB MBE Tracker, which is available for free download at FckThe-Bar.com.

To track your time, use a timer while you practice. Multiply whole minutes by 60, then add in the remaining seconds. Divide by the number of questions you answered, which gives you your average time per question.

For example, if you answered 25 questions in 45:38, your calculation would look like this:

- 45 minutes x 60 = 2,700 seconds
- 2,700 seconds + 38 seconds = 2,738 seconds
- 2,738 seconds / 25 questions = 109.52 seconds per question
- Rounded up = 110 seconds per question
- You are aiming for 108 seconds or less per question because you have 108 seconds, or 1.8 minutes, for each MBE if you are to finish in time.

As you track your MBE progress, you will be able to see how you are improving. You may find that Real Property is your weakest subject, and Evidence your strongest. Information like that can be employed as a great test-taking strategy come the bar exam. For example, if you are finding yourself running out of time on the actual MBE, spend your precious minutes answering the remaining

Evidence questions, and quickly look over the Property questions and quickly make your best guess. In this way, you will maximize your potential for earning points since you have a greater chance of getting Evidence questions correct.

SHIT LISTS

Whenever you get a practice MBE wrong, it goes on your Shit List. The concept behind the Shit List is very simple: keep track of the questions you get wrong, and go over them again later (and keep going over them until you get them correct). The FTB Shit List is available for free download at FckTheBar.com, and is shown here in a truncated version for illustration.

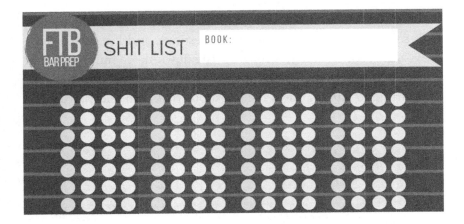

You can use the FTB Shit List with any MBE book that you select, although for obvious reasons I advocate only using a book with authentic, recent, MBE questions. Simply write in the title of the book you're using (or some other identifier) at the top where indicated so you can keep track of which questions you're practicing and tracking. On the far left column (yellow dots), write down the question number of each question that you got wrong. That question is now on your Shit List. For example (see below), let's say that I've done 20 questions in my MBE book, and I got questions 2, 3, 4, 8, 13, 19, and

20 wrong. I write down 2, 3, 4, 8, 13, 19, and 20. Now I know that I've gotten those questions wrong once.

Now let's say that the next day I pick back up and do questions 21-40 in my MBE book, and I got questions 24, 25, 32, 34, and 37 wrong. I add 24, 25, 32, 34, and 37 to the list. My Shit List is growing as I practice.

As your Shit List grows, and you progress in your MBE practice, you will want to start working through your Shit Lists. I highly, highly recommend using your Shit List for your 100 question half-length practice exams. Using only the hardest questions, which test your weakest areas, during some of your longest practice sessions, is the best way to simulate the MBE. The real MBE will feel totally manageable if you've already done your hardest work during practice.

When you finally get to the point where you use your Shit List for practice, you continue marking your incorrect answers on the list. Let's say I've just done my Shit List questions, and I've gotten questions 2, 4, 8, 20, 32, and 37 wrong. I write down those numbers again, but in the next column over. I have whittled down my Shit List, and am starting to narrow down the questions that I am really struggling with.

By seeing what rules you repeatedly answer incorrectly, you will quickly discover where you are weakest and what rules you need to learn better. You may also find that the questions you continue missing have a particular question/answer style in common (such as asking you which answer selection is NOT correct). If you find this to be the case, you know that you will have to pay extra attention to those question styles. Start noticing what you're getting hung up on.

You will find that when you're working from your Shit List, you will still keep getting some of the questions wrong, even though you've already practiced that question once, twice, even three times before. They will continue to challenge you. Once you've gotten a Shit List question correct, you don't do it again unless and until you're ready to rotate through the materials all over again from the top.

If you use the approximately 620 authentic and updated MBE questions for practice, you can easily go through them twice or three times without them losing their effectiveness. I guarantee you won't remember having done a particular question after going through 620 of them. However, you will have some familiarity, which is a result of getting used to the editorial style of the questions, which is precisely what you want to happen! The more questions you do, the more familiar they become. The more familiar they become, the better you get at understanding and answering them. It's like reading a favorite author frequently enough that you learn their "voice."

This is one of the most significant benefits of using only authentic and recent MBE questions - it familiarizes you ahead of time with the editorial style of the MBE questions you are going to see on exam day. When you first start bar prep, it might seem like fake questions by other companies are mostly the same or perhaps even indistinguishable from the real questions, but once you've done 100, 250, or 500 of them, you learn that it's simply not true. What initially may have seemed like minor or nuanced differences become huge differences over time and on the real test. Even the NCBE says not to use their older questions (which are authentic!) due to changes in format, so you better believe this makes a difference.

———

Keep Your Books "Clean"

When using your MBE books, try not to mark in them. I know some of you actively engage the MBE question by highlighting, underlining, and circling important words and phrases. If that is how you need to do MBEs to be successful, then, by all means, do what you need to do. But if you can, refrain from marking on the answer selections themselves, and if you must do so, use a pencil so you can erase the marks.

The reasoning behind this is that when you go back through and do the questions over, especially questions from your Shit Lists, your brain will look for clues as to what is the correct/incorrect answer based on the markings. Even the words and phrases you marked in the text of the question could throw you off by hinting to the correct or incorrect answer because you automatically notice those words and phrases more. It is natural for the brain to think that there is something critical about the marked words, thereby giving them more weight. Don't set yourself up to make the same MBE mistakes over and over by leaving a trail from the first time you attempted the question.

Leaving the text clean is also a good idea for economic reasons. If your books aren't marked, you can resell them later and recoup at least a portion of what you spent.

Supplementation

If you're following the "good form" steps outlined above, you should see your scores naturally improve as you progress through bar prep and practice MBEs daily. However, if you get to the point halfway through bar prep, and you do not have an average proficiency of 60% or higher, it is time to supplement your MBE prep to give you a boost. (Everyone has stronger and weaker subjects, so you might average 57% on Torts, but 65% on Evidence - in this case, your overall average is 61%, and you are progressing sufficiently at this stage.)

Law in a Flash flashcards is a great way to improve your understanding of the nuances of the MBE subjects, which will improve your MBE score. This series offers packs for each of the MBE subjects. There are five main reasons these flashcards are recommended:

- The cards are written very well and are easy to understand. There's a limited amount of information on each card, so the law is broken down into digestible increments. Plus, the subject material is very well organized, with each card building upon the prior one, walking you through the subject step-by-step.

- In addition to the cards containing the substantive material, there are many which give you hypothetical questions to test whether you fully understand the rules of law and the concepts that have been presented. They are clever questions, and you must have a real understanding of the underlying legal principles to get the question right. If you are getting the hypotheticals correct, you know you're understanding the law.

- The hypothetical cards are differentiated from the instructional cards (the instructional cards are marked with three diamonds). This permits you to skip right to the hypotheticals to test your knowledge or skip over them to get right to a substantive review.

- The material is reliable so long as you are using the most recent version. Just check the publication date.

- Of all flashcard options, none get into the minutiae of the law in the same way as the MBE does like these do. They really improve MBE understanding unlike anything else.

If you read through the flashcards, you will see your MBE score improve. You may want to get the flashcards for one or two of your worst subjects and see for yourself if it's worth the investment to get the others.

The flashcards are particularly recommended for Civil Procedure as that is the most recently added subject on the MBE and therefore is the subject with the fewest released questions from the NCBE.

The other product recommended for helping boost MBE scores if needed is *Strategies & Tactics for the MBE* by Walton and Emmanuel. This is a good book for MBE preparation because it is chock full of useful tips about how to improve your skill in answering MBE questions. It provides approaches for reading the questions and discerning the important facts, as well as analyzing the answer choices and eliminating the incorrect ones.

The real gold in this book isn't necessarily the practice questions; it's the author's advice and content *before* you get to the practice questions. Since that's where the most value lies, you can likely pick up an older copy for much less than the full retail of the newest version. There's a very high probability your law school library will have at least one copy on the shelf.

12

SHORT ANSWERS

If you are in a jurisdiction that includes a short answer component to the bar exam, then prepare for it with the same techniques as you prepare for the essays and performance tests - practice! Get as many prior exams as you can, as well as sample answers, and systematically go through them, spacing them out and increasing the difficulty as you get closer to the bar exam.

13

STUDY SCHEDULE

For the purpose of the study schedule outlined here, I will assume that you are studying for a jurisdiction which tests on essays, performance tests, and the MBE since that is the case for the majority of states. If your jurisdiction is different, you can alter the schedule to follow your own needs.

From the first day you are going to be spending your time effectively. You will be writing essays and practicing MBEs daily. You will be taking performance tests weekly. All assignments are created to fit into 4-hour Study Blocks (discussed in more detail below), and there are eighty 4-hour Study Blocks in The Klein Method, for a total of 320 hours to be spent in preparation. If you follow a full-time study schedule, you will need seven weeks to prepare. If you follow a part-time schedule, you will need twelve weeks to prepare.

Because the program is created to be completed in eighty 4-hour Study Blocks, you can break it up to fit your schedule, whatever that is. For example, if you have nothing else to do and can eat, drink, and sleep bar prep, you could do a bar exam "blitz" and do all eighty Study Blocks in four or five weeks by doing three Study Blocks each day. It's possible!

THE 4-HOUR STUDY BLOCK

When you are studying, you need to be studying. The time you spend should be completely undivided to be the most effective. Remember, this is about being smart with your time and getting the most out of it. If you spend your study time as suggested, you will know you have put in a good day's work, and you won't feel guilty or worried about going to the movies, on a date, or to that yoga class. Having that assuredness in your preparation is one of the keys to staying balanced during this process.

Remember those bold statements back at the beginning of this book about removing the pain from bar exam prep? About how you can have a different experience? You can go through the bar prep process feeling calm, confident, prepared, organized, rested, supported, positive, balanced, and enjoying your life during the process. If that is the experience you want, then you need to take seriously what I am about to tell you: It all comes down to throwing yourself into the daily Study Blocks. Whenever you're in a 4-hour Study Block, BE IN IT. Give yourself over entirely to the task in front of you without any division in your energy or attention.

The way in which you fully focus on the work at hand during those 4-hour Study Blocks is by stepping out of the world you live in and back to the raddest time of all: the 1980s. Specifically, I'm thinking of 1985 - that magical year which brought us *The Breakfast Club*, *Back to the Future*, and *The Goonies*. The year where you had access to a computer, but no internet. Back when you had to study at your desk at home, or a library because there was no neighborhood Starbucks. No cell phones, Facebook, Instagram, Snapchat, or text messages.

The world we live in today is amazing. But quite frankly, it's not going to serve you during those Study Blocks. If you want to make the most of those Study Blocks, get shit done, and then go about the rest of your day enjoying yourself with no guilt, worry, or stress about that big exam looming on the calendar, then you're going to want to go retro.

Drive yourself to a *library*. Take off your Apple Watch and leave your cell phone in your car. When you open your laptop, turn off WiFi. Now open your book, put your head down, *and work*.

I promise you - when you've completed your 4-hour Study Block, you will feel accomplished. You will have put in an honest, hard day's work, and *this is going to change your life*! You will not be tormented by the omnipresent anxiety that plagues so many of your comrades taking those commercial classes.

It's not that they aren't working hard. They are. They're very busy, frantically working, undoubtedly more hours than you are. However, they're not spending their time as effectively as you. You are maximizing your time. They probably spent those same four hours on lectures and outlines or writing out flashcards, interrupted by a bunch of notifications on their phones, a couple of coffee orders, and who knows what else. In the same amount of time, you just wrote four full-length essays and did thirty MBEs.

Let's say both you and your commercial prep class friend are both working on Evidence right now. They probably don't feel "ready" to write any essays yet because they don't "know everything" about Evidence yet. Moreover, they're probably not going to feel "ready" for a long time. They've spent the day listening to lectures or reading outlines on Evidence - all of which overwhelms them with information overload - information they don't have stored away in their memory banks. So at the end of that study day, they have a tremendous amount of anxiety because they are thinking about how much Evidence they *don't* know.

In contrast, you have just written four Evidence essays that were given on past administrations of the bar exam. These are essays which are *exactly* the same as you will be given on your exam. You have applied Evidence knowledge in a way that translates to improved performance, while only focusing on the portions of the broad topic of Evidence that actually matter. You aren't feeling "unready" for anything. You're already doing the thing that your friend is afraid to try!

You're not going to end that day worried about not knowing enough Evidence. So you can enjoy yourself at the brewery tonight with your friends as you relax and laugh. You sleep soundly, having worked hard and feeling confident in your study plan. Then you wake up refreshed and slay your day tomorrow, the day after that, and the day after that.

It is incredibly rare for us to truly give our undivided focus and attention to ANYTHING for four hours at a time. Not even movies get your attention for four hours straight. Perhaps the only thing in everyday life in which this happens is when we sleep. For obvious reasons, that happens on a subconscious level without any effort on our part.

Making yourself study for four hours straight will be difficult at first. It will feel strange. You will find yourself seeking out distractions. Just stick with it. Throw yourself into your work, resist the distraction temptation, it will become second nature, and the four hours will start to go by quickly.

As I mentioned earlier, if you follow your schedule day in and day out, you'll never feel guilty when you're not studying or when you're enjoying your life. You won't have the bar exam hanging around in the back of your mind like a big angry gorilla putting a damper on the other hours of your day. You will feel completely confident in both the *quantity* and *quality* of your studies, which gives you the freedom to engage in whatever else you decide to spend your remaining time on.

THE 4-HOUR STUDY BLOCK

For each Essay & MBE Study Block:

- The first 2.5-3 hours will be spent reading, copying, and

writing essay questions at whatever stage you are
currently working in.

- The last 1-1.5 hours of the Study Block will be spent doing
  twenty to thirty practice MBEs and reviewing your
  answers. It should take approximately thirty-six minutes
  to complete twenty MBEs, or fifty-five minutes to complete
  thirty MBEs, and you should use the remaining time to do
  the review.

For each Performance Test Study Block:
(Every 8th block)

- Practice performance tests at whatever stage you are in the
  entire 4 hours.

Stages:

- For Study Blocks 1-20, do Stage 1 work.
- For Study Blocks 21-40, do Stage 2 work.
- For Study Blocks 41-60, do Stage 3 work.
- For Study Blocks 61-80, do Stage 4 work.

TAKE A MOCK EXAM

In addition to the regular Study Blocks you will be doing for most
of bar prep, you will also want to schedule in at least one full-length
practice test. I recommend you do this around Study Blocks sixty. You
will devote four Study Blocks to the full-length test. The first day, give
yourself as much time as you will have on the actual bar exam (typically six hours broken up with a lunch break). The second day you
should do the full-length MBE, which is going to be six hours broken
up with a lunch break.

When you take your practice exam, take it seriously. You're doing
this for *your* benefit. Any shortcuts you take only result in you short-

changing yourself. Simulate the bar exam conditions the best you can.

If you are sitting for the July bar, I recommend you take the July exam from the year prior. Do not do any of those essays or performance tests as practice beforehand. Save them for your mock exam day, so it's all material you've not seen before.

If you are sitting for the February bar, I recommend you do likewise: Do the prior year's February administration, making sure you've earmarked that exam for this very purpose.

If you want the hardest MBE experience, use your mixed Shit List OR set aside 200 questions that you've never used before for this very purpose.

———

The Traditional Full-Time Study Schedule

For those of you who have the opportunity to study for the bar exam full-time in the weeks leading up to the exam, without the added stress of work or other time-consuming responsibilities, you may follow this schedule. The study schedule outlined here is based on doing twelve 4-hour Study Blocks per week. That means you will only need to work eight hours per day, Monday-Saturday. This is a steady pace. It is not extreme; you will not have a mental breakdown on this schedule. You will have time for adequate rest and whatever it is you do for relaxation (hobby, exercise, social events, etc.). Both rest and personal time are extremely important!

If you start the program seven weeks out from the bar exam, it will also give you an extra couple days of flex, which comes in handy around holidays, birthdays, sick days, etc. Or, if you end up falling behind, this schedule allows for that. You will be able to increase your daily study hours without going overboard because you have the other sixteen hours per day to work with, plus Sundays.

Nevertheless, if you follow the plan I outline, you are unlikely to need to increase your study time. That is because all your study time is being spent wisely, and you will be surprised how productive you are in those eight hours.

I recommend getting an early start to the day because you will need an early start for the actual bar exam. It's better to work on adjusting yourself now so that when it comes time for the exam your body, and more importantly your brain, is humming along at peak performance when it's go-time. Here is a sample schedule you can follow:

Monday - Saturday

- 8:00 a.m. - 10:30 a.m. Essays (2-5 essays depending on your jurisdiction and stage)
- 10:30 a.m. - 10:45 a.m. Break
- 10:45 a.m. - 12:15 p.m. 30 MBEs & Review
- 12:15 p.m. - 12:45 p.m. Lunch
- 12:45 p.m. - 3:15 p.m. Essays (2-5 essays depending on your jurisdiction and stage)
- 3:15 p.m. - 3:30 p.m Break
- 3:30 p.m. - 5:00 p.m 30 MBEs & Review

Performance Test Study Blocks

- 90-120 minutes: Performance Test (timing depending on your stage)
- 15 minutes: Break
- 90-120 minutes: Performance Test (timing depending on your stage)

Sundays - relax!

If you follow this schedule, you can see how quickly you are going to become proficient at every part of the bar exam. In just one week of following this schedule, you will have completed 330 MBEs, between twenty-two and sixty-six full-length practice essays, and two full-length performance tests! *Your skill and confidence will be through the roof by the time you take the exam.* That is what this approach is all about.

————

The Part-Time Study Schedule For Those With Other Commitments

For many of you, the challenge of studying for the bar exam will be made more difficult because you are either working full-time or have some other time-consuming commitment such as being the primary caregiver for a child. Whatever the case, you have a significantly decreased amount of time to study. If this is the situation you find yourself in, there are a few options available to you.

Regardless of which option you choose, there is good news for you despite your challenging situation. That is this: this program will give you maximum results for your study time since you will not be wasting it on anything that does not directly contribute to improving your performance on the MBE, performance test, or essays. You can rest assured that your precious time will be spent wisely.

This sample schedule works from the assumption that you have a typical forty-hour per week job (or other commitment), and you can devote one 4-hour Study Block each evening, and two 4-hour Study Blocks each weekend, for a total of seven 4-hour Study Blocks per week. This equates to twenty-eight to thirty hours per week once you consider study breaks.

Monday - Friday

- 6:00 p.m. - 8:30 p.m Essays (2-5 essays depending on your jurisdiction and stage)
- 8:30 p.m. - 8:45 p.m. Break
- 8:45 p.m. - 10:15 p.m. 30 MBEs & Review

Saturday

- 8:00 a.m. - 10:30 a.m. Essays (2-5 essays depending on your jurisdiction and stage)
- 10:30 a.m. - 10:45 a.m. Break
- 10:45 a.m. - 12:15 p.m. 30 MBEs & Review
- 12:15 p.m. - 12:45 p.m. Lunch
- 12:45 p.m. - 3:15 p.m. Essays (2-5 essays depending on your jurisdiction and stage)
- 3:15 p.m. - 3:30 p.m Break
- 3:30 p.m. - 5:00 p.m 30 MBEs & Review

Performance Test Study Blocks

- 90-120 minutes: Performance Test (timing depending on your stage)
- 15 minutes: Break
- 90-120 minutes: Performance Test (timing depending on your stage)

Sundays - relax!

I would be remiss if I didn't discuss how difficult it is to carve out thirty hours per week on top of whatever other full-time commitments you may have. Life just doesn't give that much buffer. You have to also consider things like grocery shopping, laundry, commutes, birthdays, sick days, and the occasional I'm-going-to-lose-it-and-I-don't-give-a-fuck days.

That said, I highly recommend finding a more balanced way to approach bar prep if you find yourself in this situation. Be realistic about it. I've had student who fell waaaaay behind in bar prep because life is just too busy, and they didn't get their Study Blocks in. Be conservative in your estimates and plan accordingly. Consider some of these options:

Option 1 - Cut Back

Decrease or eliminate your other commitment(s). This is obviously not going to be an option for everyone. There is a good chance that the reason you have the other commitment is that it is not optional. Perhaps you provide the sole income to support your family and cannot stop working. However, if you are a post-bar clerk with no family to support, or have a spouse who brings in an income, you have more flexibility and can eat rice and beans for a few months.

The critical thing to realize about this option is that although it is going to be uncomfortable to make adjustments and will cost you money to cut back at work, it might just be the price you will have to pay to get licensed. Depending on your situation, you may very well have to make more significant sacrifices than other people have had to make to reach the same goal. But is it worth it to get the desired result? If you knew right now that you would never pass the bar unless you cut down to part-time work, would you do it? Why take the bar and fail over and over again because you weren't willing to buckle down for three months and make the necessary sacrifice?

Many people have taken the bar two, three, four, five, or more times because each time they tried to fit bar study around their busy work schedule. There's a case at work, or a big project that needs to get done - there's always some reason not to cut back the hours. However, if they had just sucked it up, dedicated those two or three months the first time around, and *fully invested themselves* in the process they could have saved themselves so much more time in the long run.

Option 2 - Spread It Out

Skip an administration of the exam and take the following one, giving yourself more time to prepare. For some reason, unbeknownst to me, few people seem to take this route or see it as a viable strategy for passing the bar exam. Perhaps they believe it will put off obtaining their license too long, or that people will think they've given up. Another possible reason is that people think it's simply unnecessary and they will be able to scrounge together enough time to prepare despite their other commitments.

If you are unable to remove some or all of your commitments and are relegated to studying in the late evening hours after you've returned home from work or put the kids to bed, consider whether the time you're finding for study is even *effective*. You are probably physically and mentally exhausted. You likely have little to no time to put into maintaining even a single personal relationship, making you feel even more drained and isolated. You won't be able to carve out any time to spend on yourself or activities that rejuvenate you, such as exercise, thereby adding to your stress and exhaustion.

How long could you operate at this pace before the study time you do get becomes utterly worthless? Your ability to concentrate, build mental stamina, put forth a good effort, and retain information will be close to zero. It ends up being a waste of time and almost entirely ineffective.

Instead of this impossible schedule, why not spread bar prep out over a longer period of time? By spreading out your study schedule, you will be able to maintain a steady, effective pace. You will be under less stress and have some time for important things like personal time and exercise. Do not undervalue these things - they will help you study better.

The most important benefit of this option, however, is that it gives you the amount of time you really need to make sure you are adequately prepared for the exam and will not have to retake it.

Option 3 - Custom Tailor

Because there are always going to be unique circumstances among those who are studying for the bar exam, there are going to be unique solutions, as well. Depending on your situation, you may have to tailor the above suggestions for the best fit or come up with your own creative solutions. In the end, it's all about taking a realistic look at what your circumstances are and setting yourself up for success on the bar exam. You need to ensure you are giving yourself enough time to adequately prepare. Plus, the time you commit needs to be quality, so you must be taking care of yourself physically, mentally, and emotionally. Know what pace you can commit to, what sacrifices you and your family can make, and create a schedule that works.

14

YOUR BAR PREP LIFESTYLE

Lifestyle is an important factor affecting your success on the bar exam. For many would-be lawyers, this is a big challenge. It is no secret that law school is highly competitive and extremely stressful. The coping mechanisms that many law students develop during those three to four years may be useful in the short-term, but dangerous in the long-term.

Smoking, drinking, poor eating habits, lack of exercise, cynicism, and sometimes even drug use, become the bedfellows of law students across the nation. Those law students become the local bar: first-year associates, prosecutors, solo practitioners, partners, and even judges.

Although these poor lifestyle choices may be effective to help get you through a week of finals in law school, or a big project at work, they are destructive in the long-term. Studying for the bar exam is the quintessential "marathon," and thus you need a different approach to getting yourself through it successfully.

The topic of lifestyle is wide-ranging and encompasses myriad sub-topics. There is so much that can be said about improving lifestyle, as there are countless factors that affect our daily lives. But for the purposes of this topic, only a few basic ones will be mentioned here as an integral part of a successful study plan. No, you don't have to quit smoking or give up the bottle. In fact, I would advise against a significant life change like that while you are preparing for the bar. There are a few basic lifestyle tweaks you can make, however, that will help you get through this period in your life and make your bar prep more successful.

1. EAT BETTER

If you have poor eating habits, you don't need to overhaul your entire diet and go raw. However, you can make a few small changes that will make a big difference for you. Make small changes like switching out soda and so-called "energy" drinks for water, pack your lunches and skip the drive-thru, and eat fresh fruit or trail mix instead of a candy bar as a snack. Do your best to provide your body with nourishment so it can serve you well during this period (after all, your brain is part of your body!).

These are all the common-sense things that we all know we should do yet still skip over. Small changes like these will go a long way to providing your body with nutrition and sustained energy. Just getting rid of some of that toxic sugar will help your energy and mental clarity improve. Something as simple as taking a daily supplement is a small change you can make to really help your body get what it needs.

There are many ways in which you can make better choices about what you eat and drink. These are just a few simple suggestions about how to substitute poor eating habits that drain your body of nutrients and energy for ones that provide nutrition and fuel for your demanding lifestyle.

If you know that your eating habits need an overhaul and constitute a significant obstacle to your success in studying, then spend some time looking into what you need to do to make positive changes in a way that supports your bar exam goals but does not overshadow them.

2. Sleep Better

Getting adequate sleep sounds so easy. Who doesn't want to sleep in another thirty minutes? However, getting enough sleep isn't possible when you're sabotaging it by your bad habits. Even if you only get six hours a night, the quality will be better if you get the basics down. Again, none of this ground-breaking information and you've likely heard it before. Yet *implementing it* is the only way it will help you:

- Have a regular sleep schedule - i.e., go to bed and wake up at the same time every day. This includes weekends! Your body thrives when it has sleep regularity.

- Don't have a television in your room or fall asleep on the couch watching TV.

- Don't end your evening watching the news, reading horror stories about the bar exam, or putting any other disturbing thoughts in your brain. Fill your mind with peaceful and uplifting thoughts that won't torment you as you sleep.

- Put aside your worries somehow - whether you need to jot down a to-do list for tomorrow, pray, journal, meditate or call your mom - just get them off your chest so you can sleep as stress-free as possible.

- Make your bedroom conducive to sleeping. Keep your room comfortable and get fresh airflow. Have good window coverings to keep it dark during sleeping hours. Use a fan or a sleep machine if you like to have white noise in the background. Get rid of the jarring light emanating from your clock and phone by turning it away from you or putting it face down. Put your phone on Do Not Disturb. The notifications can wait.

- Don't work on your laptop or pay your bills while sitting in bed, especially right before sleep! Don't bring your bar prep books into bed. Don't study there. Your bed is for sleep and sex only.

3. PERSONAL TIME

Personal time is time that has no utility except to feel good. It is time that is not spent taking care of responsibilities, helping other people, or doing anything else altruistic. The truth is, you need some time every week that is completely selfish. You should do something that is only aimed at making you happy.

I think everyone pretty much understands the value in this: if you get a chance to be selfish and do what makes you happy every once in a while, you will feel rejuvenated instead of deprived. Then you will be able to go back and face your responsibilities with renewed energy and vigor. Even if you're not getting enough personal time to feel renewed, it might be just enough to blow off some steam and keep you from going over the edge.

Please don't mistake me. I absolutely do not think that doing things for the sole purpose of making yourself happy is selfish. However, plenty of people do. If the idea of spending time on yourself, especially when you probably barely spend any time on your closest friends and family right now sounds incredibly selfish to you, then hear me out: it is not selfish! I give you permission to take that time for yourself.

I promise you - it. is. necessary. Get that mani/pedi. Have that poker night. Watch a movie. Read that novel. Shoot some hoops. Go to the wine tasting. Whatever it is, it is necessary. Take care of yourself. You cannot perform on the bar exam as your best self if only a shell of a person shows up on exam day.

Moreover, while you're doing it, DO NOT THINK ABOUT THE BAR EXAM. If you are doing the work day in and day out, you have nothing to feel guilty about. The work is getting done, and when you're done for the day, you're done. Bar exam brain gets turned off.

4. EXERCISE

Just as with your eating habits, it is not necessary to make a drastic change to your physical activity level. If you are already somewhat physically active, then that's fine. But if you are not physically active at all, it is really important you find something active that you can enjoy. The goal is not to get bikini-body ready or carve out a six-pack for yourself by the bar exam. No, the goal is simply to release some stress and tension from your body. Physical activity has the added benefit of improving your memory, among other things.

So whether you walk on the beach for thirty minutes, dance at the club, mountain climb, or roller skate with the kids, get your body moving. You should be able to find something that not only gets your body moving, but is also something you enjoy, look forward to, and is at an exertion level appropriate for you.

In addition to finding a physical activity to engage in regularly, don't forget to get your body moving during little study breaks. Stand up from your chair and stretch your body once an hour. Sit outside for five minutes every couple of hours and breathe the fresh air deeply. Go for a ten-minute stroll during your lunch break. Small doses of physical movement while you study will keep you fresh and help your concentration tremendously.

5. RELATIONSHIPS

It is extremely important to maintain at least one relationship that nourishes you. I know that almost all relationships are put on hold when you are preparing for the bar exam, especially if you have other commitments and responsibilities. However, you need to have at least one relationship which you can lean on for support during this time. This might even mean that the relationship is relatively one-sided for this short period of time. If it is a quality relationship, that person will probably understand your temporary selfishness and be willing to give that support.

Your idea of a supportive relationship might be the one you have with your cat (since you can be utterly selfish), a therapist, or even a bar exam forum where others are able to commiserate with your struggles. The important thing is that you share your frustrations, stress, fears, etc., with someone. You need to be able to express your challenges and receive understanding, support, and encouragement in return.

6. MENTAL ATTITUDE

The last lifestyle factor that you need to consider is your mental attitude. In other words, you need to make a concerted effort to control what you feed your mind. Whether you know it or not, what you think about, and the worldview that you have, have a massive impact on your life.

The saying "you are what you eat" is as true in the area of your thought life as it is for your physical body. If you constantly believe negative things are going to happen, or things are going to go wrong, I bet they often do! If you see the positive in everything and believe that good things are coming your way, I bet you're right most of the time.

Not to sound Pollyanna-ish, but a positive mental outlook truly is a powerful thing. It's not about rainbows, butterflies, and being out of check with reality. It's about realizing that our life experience is created in our minds. Use the power of your mental attitude to create for yourself a positive, confident, and successful bar exam experience. You're going to go through it anyway. Go through it having the best possible outlook and experience that you can.

Let's get really crazy for a minute and think about how you could even be grateful that you're taking the bar exam! First of all, you won the genetic lottery if you were born with the mental faculties that have allowed you to pursue this career choice. You live in a nation with enough infrastructure to sustain higher learning institutions in which you were able to learn from brilliant minds. You have enough money to pay the fees to take the exam. You get to spend countless hours studying instead of walking miles every day to get some dirty drinking water. Your body allows you to sit at a desk for hours on end instead of lying in a hospital bed praying for an organ donor. I could go on and on.

The point is, you choose your attitude. If no one has ever told you before, the attitude you choose has incredible power over your daily experience. So I advocate you decide to throw yourself into the process. Give yourself to the work. With each essay you write, think of how exciting it is that you are weeks away from finally taking the exam that stands as a doorway to your dreams. Realize that your years of hard work are coming to a head and every MBE you do is one less MBE standing between you and your swearing-in ceremony. Visualize that moment. Think about what you will wear. Who will be there with you? How will you celebrate after? Can you imagine what it's going to feel like the first time you receive a piece of mail with "Esq." after your name? Or when the court calls you "counsel" for the first time? Or when you walk into the courtroom, past the gallery, and take a seat at counsel table?

Really feel it. Sit with that excitement. Put as much detail and anticipation and energy behind it as you can, and you will be amazed at how well bar prep will go. You will be amazed at how confident you'll be when you walk into that exam room.

The bar exam is as much mental as it is anything else, so align your thoughts with the results you want. You can feel defeated before you even walk in to take the exam, or you can jump out of bed on exam day with ferocity, ready to slay that bar exam like the boss you are. The choice is yours to make.

15

EXAM DAY

Plan your exam day strategy. Compile all your supplies ahead of time and practice with them during your mock exam. You will find out what you forgot to include and what you might not need with you after all. The last thing you want to happen is to forget to bring something or bring something not permitted in the testing center.

Make sure to check with your jurisdiction to find out what the examination administration rules, policies, and procedures are. Find out which items are and are not permitted in the exam room. After you have compiled your supplies, put them all in a gallon size Ziploc bag. This will save you the hassle of having the proctors go through your items to make sure you brought no prohibited items. They will be able to easily see what you've brought and move on.

Check your laptop before you leave home. Have your battery completely charged and bring your power cord.

The Lunch Break

Making sure you get a good lunch is as much a part of doing well on the bar exam as any other part. You will be mentally exhausted (especially on MBE day), as well as physically. You will need to eat enough to fill you up, but not so much that you become groggy. It is recommended that you always pack a good lunch. Even if you are planning on eating at a nearby restaurant, you must be prepared for the worst-case scenario. Should something go wrong, you need to have a meal available.

Unless you are familiar with the restaurants near the testing center, it is much safer to brown bag it. Homemade meals have a significantly smaller chance of giving you food poisoning or disagreeing with your stomach. Really simple meals, like peanut butter and jelly sandwiches, are a foolproof option. Keep it simple during the bar exam, and save your chef-tastic skills for another day.

In addition to having your lunch planned out, have your lunch strategy in place as well. What I mean by your lunch strategy is this: where are you going to eat your lunch? With whom (if anybody) are you going to eat it? What are you going to do or think about during the lunch break? Would you do better eating alone in your car, or do you want to re-hash all the juicy test details with a friend? Is your significant other going to come to meet you for your lunch break? Are you going to stretch your legs in a nearby park? Do you want to take a power nap in your car? If so, do you have a sure-fire way to ensure you won't oversleep?

BE CONSIDERATE

Think about the other test-takers, as well. No one should be able to tell that you ate garlic at lunch. Or what brand of perfume you wear, for that matter. The only scent, if any, your fellow test-takers should smell is the soap you showered with that morning and the clean scent of freshly laundered clothes. Nor should you walk about the testing center during the lunch break or after the exam exclaiming what you believe to have been the right answers to the questions. If you have a friend who is agreeable to hash it out, then do so privately. Don't assume the others want to hear it.

Practice The Exam Day

Make sure you are prepared for exam day in every way. You should have already done a dry run with your supplies on the mock exam and have them ready to go for test day. Make your plan to meet up with friends when you arrive at the test center or find a quiet place to be by yourself. Get as much control over your environment as possible on test day by having your plan in place. It will cut down on test anxiety and make you feel more comfortable.

If at all possible, go check out the test center before the exam. Walk around, get familiar with the rooms and the hallways; note the bathroom locations. You might be surprised how much anxiety you will cut out by just having seen the test center before exam day. Drive to the test center on the same days, and at the same times, you are going to be driving on exam day. Find out what the traffic situation will be like on the exact route you plan to take. Carry some cash just in case. Find at least one alternate route. Locate two different parking lots. You don't want to experience any of these things for the first time on exam day.

If Something Goes Wrong...

If something goes wrong on exam day, do everything you can not to panic. Although it is a perfectly natural reaction, it is utterly useless. It will only make things worse. Keep your cool and get through the rest of the day the best you can. The sooner you can solve whatever problem you're facing, and get your head back in the game, the less damage you will suffer.

No matter what happens, do not give up! Ever! At the time, things may seem so catastrophic that you could never recover, and you may think you will inevitably fail. Don't let those thoughts keep you from pushing through and continuing to do your best. There is more than one story where a test taker was convinced they had messed up so badly that they were sure to fail, so they threw in the towel and walked out. When their scores came back, they found they were actually on track to pass and would have if only they had seen it through and finished the exam.

At the very least, even if you did suffer a deadly blow, keep going so you can benefit from the exam. You have paid a good amount of money just to sit in that room and take that exam. If you do fail, you are going to get back your scores and written answers. Use that to your benefit. See how you scored on the sections you did make it through. Did you do better on one essay than you felt like you had? Did you have a weak score on a performance test you thought you nailed? You are going to benefit from this information the next time around, so don't throw the learning opportunity away.

16

A WORD TO THE REPEATERS

S o you failed the bar exam. So what?

So you failed the bar exam *a bunch of times*. Again I say, *so what*?

The reason I say "so what?" is not to be flippant. I promise. In fact, not only do I feel for you, I understand what it feels like to fail. To have that heaviness like a boulder dropping in the pit of your stomach. The disbelief when you read the computer screen. Wondering how you're supposed to announce your defeat to everyone in your life in a way that makes it less awkward *for them*. Realizing that although you tried to prepare yourself for the possibility you might fail so as to draw the sting, it made no difference at all because it still feels so shameful and painful. Deep down you were really hoping and expecting to see your name on the pass list.

I get it.

But here's why I say "so what?" You probably don't really know (1) why you failed, or (2) that it is almost always fixable.

Having failed in the past does NOT mean you are destined to fail again and forever. You probably will continue to fail if you do not get down to the root of the cause and take the appropriate remedial action. If you can figure out the one or more causes of your poor performance, and resolve those issues, you can change your outcome. However, you must change your input first. You cannot do the same thing you did last time and think that by just doing more of it, you will have a different result. No. You must (1) identify and (2) correct.

People fail the bar exam for a whole host of reasons. Here's a list of some. As you read through, some might resonate with you as having played a part in your own experience. Keep in mind that some of the items on the list will sufficiently derail your bar exam all on their own. However, many are the types of things that compound with others on the list - none of which doomed you in isolation, but came together to cause a sub-par performance overall. Make a note of each and every reason which resonates with you. The best approach is to correct each and every issue - even if it seems a small one in the grand scheme of things.

This book doesn't (and can't) deal with every possible cause of your prior exam failure. For example, if you have undiagnosed ADD, you need to talk to a doctor about diagnosis and management options. However, this book does go into depth about how to improve your performance on the bar exam tasks. If you take the actions recommended and follow the program, you ought to be able to correct those issues and learn to perform the bar exam tasks like the graders want them performed.

1. UNDIAGNOSED CONDITIONS SUCH AS ADD OR ADHD

These are very real neurological conditions that affect one's ability to focus and perform. And don't think that because you are a highly educated, ambitious, and successful individual that you can't have these conditions. It is not uncommon for people with these conditions to be super successful in spite of these challenges because they figure out ways to compensate as they go through life. Successful and brilliant people often go through life undiagnosed.

2. Reading and writing challenges such as dyslexia and related conditions

Like ADD and ADHD, these types of conditions are real, are not your fault, are nothing to be ashamed of, and do not have anything to do with your intelligence. In fact, it's probably likely that you are just as, if not more, intelligent than your contemporaries if you have one of these conditions.

3. Failure to seek or obtain accommodations.

If you have a condition which can affect your ability to perform the bar exam under normal conditions equally with other examinees, then please seek an accommodation.

4. Slow typing

If you have never mastered keyboarding skills, you are really at a disadvantage on the bar exam (assuming you are not a hand-writer). There are typing speed tests online for free, such as www.typingtest.com that takes only a minute to perform. I had one client who struggled with this. If your typing speed is not at least forty-five words per minute, you could benefit from practicing and improving this skill to get through more content on your exam.

5. Medical issues

Medical issues are varied and could affect you in many ways. From something as simple as an issue causing you to need to take multiple bathroom breaks which eat up your time, to taking medication which causes your mind to be cloudy or groggy. It could be an issue which required you to spend a lot of time in the hospital or going to medical appointments instead of studying.

6. Personal stressors

There are so many things that happen in life which cause inner personal turmoil. These types of things don't usually wait until we have the time to handle them. They happen when they happen. They could be anything: your partner ending the relationship, being diagnosed with an illness, a loved one being diagnosed with an illness, your dog dying, your house burning down, the list is almost endless. When you are going through a dark time in your life, it is extremely difficult to focus on something like the bar exam. And that's not to say that you *should be* focused on the bar exam if you're dealing with something like this.

The point is that it is extremely difficult, if even possible, to do both. Even when the stressors are happy ones, such as welcoming a child or getting married, it is tough to devote the necessary energy and focus on that personal situation *and* the bar exam. Your heart and mind are understandably pre-occupied with this very important other thing, even if you are trying to focus on the books in front of you.

7. External stressors and responsibilities

Many people prepare for the bar exam while also juggling some other very important balls in the air that they don't have the luxury of putting aside for a few months. Common ones are: a full-time job, caring for children or aging parents, moving houses, etc. These are different from the personal stressors just mentioned in that they are more of a time stressor, and do not create as much emotional upset. Usually, when you're dealing with one of these, you have a difficult time carving out the time to study and are constantly carrying around an anxious, busy feeling. However, when you do get the time with your books, you can put your mental focus on the task at hand.

8. EXAM DAY PROBLEMS

These are myriad. It could be anything from falling ill during the exam, a fender bender on the drive there, forgetting the power cord to your laptop and having to switch to hand-writing mid-exam, forgetting your money and not being able to buy a lunch (low blood sugar anyone?), your significant other breaking up with you the day of the exam, or even going into labor (true story! Google it!). Whatever random curveball life can throw at you, the day of the bar exam is just as good a day as any. You can be cautious and be as prepared as possible, but certain circumstances just can't be foreseen or controlled.

9. EXAM ANXIETY

There are plenty of clever and capable people who have legitimate exam anxiety to deal with. I think most people can relate to the onset of symptoms one might experience when you have to give an important presentation or speech in front of a group of people. Similarly, your mind might start racing, or go blank, or become overwhelmed by negative self-talk. Physical symptoms like upset stomach, dry mouth, pounding heart, sweaty palms, or a nervous bladder might also come into play. If exam anxiety is an issue for you, it will be critical that you practice going to the testing center, seeing the testing center, visualizing yourself successfully and calmly taking the exam in that space, learning ways to calm yourself when anxiety creeps in and perhaps discussing with your doctor whether medication would be appropriate or helpful.

10. LAPTOP FAILURE

Ugh. This is a dreaded one because there's little that can be done to predict, prevent, or mitigate an unexpected technology failure. It can happen to anyone!

11. NIGHT OWL

If you're a night owl, which many people are, then you are simply not going to be operating at peak performance during the hours of the bar exam, especially the morning hours. You want to - you *need to* - bring your A-game into the bar exam. No matter how early you go to bed the night before, if it's not your daily habit to be awake and firing neurons by exam time, then your body and brain are going to begrudgingly comply with your demands of them on exam day. Your brain is simply not going to be giving its peak performance unless it is conditioned to be doing so at that hour.

When you're a month out from exam day, start going to bed and waking up at the same time you will be on exam day, and be consistent about it. Get your body and brain primed to slay at the right time of day!

12. CHANGING HABITS

Did you decide to quit smoking during bar prep? Bad idea. Go ahead and kick the bad habit... the day after the bar. Look, you've got an unhealthy habit, and it's admirable you want to make a change. However, you've got bigger fish to fry (at least more immediate fish to fry). Keep your bad habit. Keep all habits that would be more disruptive than beneficial to change during these couple of months. Deal with them later. Don't do yourself a disservice by not having that smoke break you so desperately need during lunch. If nicotine is going to get you through exam day, then, by all means, use nicotine!

13. NOT AT YOUR PEAK PHYSICALLY

Whether your brain is groggy because you're a night owl, you didn't get to eat lunch, and your blood sugar is crashing, you're getting over a stomach bug, and your body is still weak and run down, whatever it is... it affects your performance. Some of these issues can be planned for, but not all. Do what you can in advance to get your physical body on board with your goal, and do your best if something unexpected happens.

14. LACK OF BALANCE

There is something to be said for finding a balance in the weeks and months that lead up to the bar exam. Burnout is a real issue, and if you don't incorporate one or more ways to release tension and rejuvenate yourself through this time period, then it's going to be to your detriment. You are a multi-faceted and complex creature. You cannot hyper-focus on only one facet for months at a time and think that you will be able to perform at your peak. Your best performance requires all facets humming along in synchronicity. Fight for the balance from the start, and maintain it as a core part of your bar prep strategy.

15. NOT ENOUGH STUDYING

There's really nothing that can make up for lack of study. There just isn't. Even if you're doing a program like this one which requires you spend time on only the most useful tasks, you still have to get them done. If you don't get through the material, no study plan is going to work. Only you know the reason why you didn't get the work done. It could be an issue of procrastination (a biggie!), work obligations - the list is endless. What matters is that you have a raw, honest conversation with yourself about why you didn't get the work done and then make a plan for how to avoid that situation in the future.

16. NOT ENOUGH PRACTICE TESTS

So many people fall into the trap of putting off taking practice tests until they learn the law better or have it memorized. I hope I already harped on this idea enough to make it clear that this is a humongous and fatal error. You will never "feel ready." Do it anyway. Get on the horse right from the start and make yourself do it. Your first essays will be ugly as fuck. No doubt. That's okay. You want to struggle through that now, so those ugly essays aren't what you are handing in to the bar graders! Doing practice tests are what make you ready. It's not the other way around.

17. WASTING TIME ON INEFFECTIVE "STUDYING"

If you are reading outlines, listening to lectures, memorizing mnemonics, writing out flashcards, or any other such things, then you have wasted your time while also making yourself believe you have made progress. I'm sorry to say that unless what you just spent your time on has improved your *performance* on the bar exam, it was a complete waste. So even if it did improve your performance incrementally, it was much less effective than another task (practice test) which could have given you more bang for your buck. You only have so much time and so much energy. Spend it where you'll get the most improvement.

18. POOR MBE PERFORMANCE

If you have failed because of a poor MBE score, then you may have a problem with test-taking mechanics on that portion of the exam. What I mean by mechanics is perhaps you are not reading questions closely enough and are skimming over critical information. Or perhaps you are getting bogged down and take too much time per question, which relegates you to filling in all the 'C' bubbles for the last ten questions. Or maybe you can't commit to one answer and often mark the question to return to at the end of the exam, but you run out of time or didn't find all the marked questions. Implementing better strategies and practicing MBEs with them will help fix these types of issues.

19. NOT UNDERSTANDING THE MBE SUBJECTS IN ENOUGH DEPTH

If your poor MBE score isn't because of a mechanical type issue described above, and instead is just simply you not knowing the right answer, then you need to learn the substantive material better. The MBE tests nuances in the law, not the broad strokes. You need to have a firm grasp of the rules in these subjects, and you need to be able to think objectively about the questions. Do not go with your gut on the MBE. Learn the law cold. I highly recommend trying the *Law in a Flash* flashcards, as they walk you through the law in a detailed fashion that is comparable to the level of distinction that the MBE tests.

20. ISSUE SPOTTING

If you failed because you didn't write about legal issues presented, then you need more practice and using sample answers will be a big benefit to you. You will see what issues should be spotted when certain types of fact patterns are presented. Also, a tip that you might find helpful is to remember that if an issue floated through your mind as you read the fact pattern or as you were writing your answer, then it most likely should be addressed in your answer. It might not be a major issue, but if you thought of it, the bar graders probably want to know that you did. Unless you write it down, they don't know you considered it.

Remember, the fact patterns are designed to elicit legal issues. If they didn't want you to think about that legal issue that just floated through your brain, they wouldn't have included those specific facts in the question!

21. CONCLUSORY STATEMENTS

If you are being conclusory in your analyses, you likely don't know it. Being conclusory is one of those poor habits about which people have little to no self-awareness. I addressed this earlier in the book, but being conclusory is usually just a result of you failing to write down all the reasoning steps that your brain is making. You are usually skipping over the parts where your brilliant brain has made its logical deductions, and you assume the reader has also made those deductions. However, you cannot do that. It's like when your math teacher said to "show the math." You have to get nitty-gritty with it.

Copying sample answers will provide you with example after example of legal analyses which are not conclusory. As you go through the answers, you will be led through a legal analysis just as you must learn to do. You will begin to see the problem and model your writing after these superior writing samples in the process, which will likely fix the issue.

22. Omitting Facts

You might skip facts because you are anxious and aren't retaining the information, or are in a rush and read through too fast, or don't realize that all the facts are presented for a reason. A quick tip is to read the fact pattern, read the call of the question, then re-read the fact pattern again. Alternatively, try re-reading the fact pattern when you're getting close to finishing your essay just to make sure you cull every fact and weave them into your analysis before you move on and it's too late.

23. Organization

The bar graders are not going to hunt for your legal knowledge. If your answer is disorganized, disjointed, an unending block of text, or makes it difficult to see your capabilities, then you're unlikely to get credit even if the answer is hidden in a mess somewhere. Make it easy on them. Use space between paragraphs. Number or letter your points. Underline. Italicize. Capitalize. Use all the visual cues in your arsenal to make your brilliant legal answer jump out at the grader! Follow the call of the question or the prompt if it provides an organizational structure.

24. Timing Issues

If you run out of time on the exam, then you have to simply hold your feet to the fire when you practice. Do not write a magnum opus on essay one at the cost of being able to write a passing answer on essay six. It's not worth it and it won't even out. Write a comprehensive (not exhaustive!) answer within your time constraints on each and every essay or performance test. The same goes for the MBE. Spending more time on a particularly long or difficult MBE does not get you more points than the short or easy MBEs.

Be a time fanatic. Stick to your timing constraints when you practice. If you give yourself extra time during practice, you will be habituating yourself to fail on the real exam!

25. Stamina

The bar exam is a beast. It's a long two days! Uninterrupted and complete concentration is difficult to maintain for hours on end, yet that's exactly what you're going to have to do. If you have not become used to this during bar prep, especially if you have not forced yourself to take a full mock exam, you are going to hit a big fat wall on exam day. You just will. How much that wall hurts will depend on how much you've prepared yourself for the mental stamina required ahead of time.

This is a huge reason why I feel so strongly about unplugging during study time. It's a shock to your system to go four straight hours without any internet or electronics. It really is. Stamina issues come to light when you combine technology withdrawal with uninterrupted mental exertion. You will find out how difficult it is for your brain not to have constant interruptions, breaks, and rewards such as notifications from Facebook or a new SMS. When your brain is used to all these micro-breaks, it gets a ton of little opportunities to refresh itself. However, none of that will be available on exam day, so your brain will be exhausted.

Build up its stamina in advance, so you do not suffer the consequences of it not performing well when it's most fatigued at the end of the exam.

26. Intelligence

There's a possibility you're not smart enough to provide passing answers on the bar exam in the time allotted. However, as you may have figured out by now, I think it's a very unlikely possibility. You've gotten yourself through law school. I believe everyone has their own type of genius (Albert Einstein said: "Everybody is a genius. But if you judge a fish by its ability to climb a tree, it will live its whole life believing that it is stupid."), and perhaps your genius isn't the legal type. But I highly doubt it. All the signs point to you being more than capable enough in the gray matter department. Even if you're on the left side of the bell curve and need to take the bar exam multiple times, you can improve by getting better at the bar exam tasks and ultimately clear this hurdle.

———

Here's the thing. I've just listed twenty-six reasons why you might have failed. There are literally dozens of reasons that could have caused you to fail either in isolation or in combination with other reasons. Only one of those is the possibility that you're just not smart enough. ONE.

Moreover, by this point, you already know how I feel about what the statistical probability is that that is the reason you have failed in the past. It's just not that likely someone who has achieved as much as you have and worked as hard as you have for as long as you have can't pass this exam. It really, truly, isn't likely. So I hope reading through this list has helped you to see that in a very clear and very real way.

The fact that you failed the bar exam one or more times probably torments you and feels like an unshakable label. It might feel like you're wearing a scarlet letter. You probably say things to yourself like:

- I can't believe I didn't pass.

- I'm the only one of my friend group who failed.

- I worked just as hard as they did.

- I can't believe I failed but [*insert name of class goof-off here*] passed!

- I took [*insert name of big bar prep company here*] and did everything they said so why did I fail?

- I paid a ton of money for [*insert name of bar exam tutor here*] and even *they* couldn't help me!

- I feel so humiliated I failed; I don't understand what I did wrong?!

- My bar grader was having a bad day and took it out on me.

- Did my bar grader even *read* my essays?

- My family is so ashamed of me.

- I lost a job because I failed.

- On and on and on the negative self-talk goes.

Right now, I want you to REALLY focus on what I'm about to tell you. Really hear me. If you listen to what I am about to explain to you, it will do wonders for your ability to succeed on the bar exam.

NONE OF YOUR BLAMING, REGRET, SHAME, EMBARRASSMENT, DEPRESSION, DREAD, DOUBTS, ANXIETY, FEAR, OR ANY OTHER NEGATIVITY IS GOING TO DO A DAMN THING FOR YOU.

Stop beating yourself up. Stop thinking thoughts that are 100% unhelpful. If you get on that train of thought, you already know where it's going to take you. And let me ask you, have you ever felt anything other than helpless, depressed, and overwhelmed when you think those thoughts?

You have got to put your big kid pants on and take control over the situation. Take control over your mind. It ALL starts there. No longer will you board the train of negativity. If you've told yourself a story that you aren't smart enough and are incapable of passing, you're doing yourself an incredible disservice. Because not only is that very likely *untrue*, but it strips away all your power. Because if you're just plain dumb, what can be done about that? Nothing. If you tell yourself that you are going to fail again - guess what? - you will find a way to prove yourself right.

Instead of believing that you're not capable of passing the bar exam due to some innate deficiency, take the time to (1) identify the real reasons you failed, and (2) correct the causes you can fix (and minimize the causes you can't change). Once you do that, all of a sudden retaking the bar exam is a whole new game. You are not predestined to fail again. You can have a completely different outcome if you change your input. Now you have the power to change! Now your focus is on something that will actually benefit you.

In addition to taking the steps to identify and remedy your reasons for failing, which is a practical and productive way to focus your time, you should also overhaul your bar exam mindset and thought patterns. If I had the power to control your mind, I would make it so that you didn't have the ability to even consider the possibility that you might fail again. You are destined to pass. You can stop worrying about the bar exam right now.

Start thinking about the bar exam in a positive light and truly get excited about it. It will feel like an impossible task at first, but anytime you can choose a thought that feels *slightly better* than the negative one you started with, go with it. Over time, your positivity will increase, and your happy thoughts and beliefs about the bar exam will help you actually achieve that result.

Spend time in bed each night before you go to sleep, right after you wake up, or during meditative time or journaling time intentionally thinking positive and supportive thoughts. There are so many reasons to have gratitude. Seek them out.

Here are some ideas to get you started:

- I'm so glad I'm finally at the stage where all my years of education have culminated into finally taking this one last test that will allow me to start living my dream as an attorney.

- I'm so thankful that I was led to this book which helped me see the bar exam in a new way and to understand the changes I need to make to pass now.

- I know exactly what I need to be doing to prepare for the exam and I know it's going to be a game-changer!

- It's going to be so amazing when I see my name on the pass list.

- I want [name] to be the first person I tell when I pass - I can't wait to see the look on their face!

- I'm going to throw the biggest party after I get sworn in.

- I can't wait to buy a killer suit for my first day of work as an attorney.

- I know exactly where I'm going to hang my certificate.

- It feels good to have a study plan I'm confident in.

- I know that every piece of information stored in my brain is going to come to me effortlessly when I need to recall it on the exam.

- Everything is going to go smoothly on the bar exam.

- All my hard work is going to be worth it to see that bar card in my wallet.

- I can't wait to see "Esquire" after my name.

- I can't wait to sit at counsel table and hear the judge call me "counsel."

- I feel so good having spent today making real progress.

- This is a new day, a new bar exam experience, and it feels amazing to know I'm going to pass!

It is a constant practice to catch your negative thoughts (they become so habitual and chronic that we often don't even notice they're happening anymore) and to intentionally change them to something more productive. But do it. It gets easier. If you consistently tell yourself "I'm going to pass," then your brain believes it. And if your brain believes it, *it calms the fuck down*. A calm brain allows you to: sleep at night, reduce anxiety, improve memory, and perform better on the exam! These are all critically important for your success on the exam. So your telling yourself that you're going to pass will *actually help you* achieve that outcome!

As I wrap up this section, I hope you have had a complete shift in the way you think about not only your past exam experience but also how you feel about the exam you are getting ready to take. This is a new day. You know so many things you didn't before. You are learning new and effective techniques. You have a plan to implement.

I challenge you to NEVER, from this moment forward, entertain the idea that you might not pass the bar exam. Create a new mindset and set your intention. Think and speak only of bar exam success. See yourself from the other side of the bar exam, when you are seated at counsel table. That is where you belong.

17

FOR ADDITIONAL SUPPORT

I f reading this unorthodox book about how to prepare for the bar exam resonates with you, and you think one or more of the approaches presented in its pages will be helpful to you, then you have options for how to implement them.

CHERRY-PICK

The first option is to cherry-pick your favorite ideas and add them to whatever bar prep strategy you've decided is best for you. Perhaps you are taking a big name commercial prep class. That's totally fine! You don't have to scrap that plan to benefit from these ideas! Plenty of people find success on the bar exam with those kinds of companies. However, by adding one or two of my strategies into that program, you'll find that you're more productive with your time and can more quickly improve your performance.

If I had to pick one thing for everyone to implement that would give them the absolute most bang for their buck, it would be this: start practicing essays and performance tests NOW. *Before you feel even the slightest bit ready.*

If I got to pick a second thing for everyone to implement on top of that, it would be to *completely unplug* during your study time and FOCUS on the task at hand while you're studying. Just do the damn thing.

And if I were being greedy, and got to pick a third thing to add to the pile, I'd choose for everyone to focus on mindset: to never consider failure as a possibility, and to *get really fucking excited about how you're about to pass the bar exam.*

Bootstrap It!

Another option, which will resonate with all my scrappy brothers and sisters out there is to DIY it! You've just learned the system and where to source all your materials. Now all you have to do is get your hands on them (which shouldn't cost very much at all!). Get all the free resources from FckTheBar.com, and sit down with a glass of wine while you create your detailed calendar. Then you just need to wake up every day and do the damn thing.

If you are the bootstrapping kind of person, then this might be the perfect option for you. Just make sure you truly know yourself and the type of environment in which you thrive. I'm sure you are very capable, but if you struggle with discipline, or perhaps you feel isolated if you work alone for too long, then you might need something with more support, structure, or accountability.

Work with Me

You may be entirely on board with the ideas and concepts of the program outlined in this book, but have no interest in having it fall on your shoulders to take these ideas and turn them into a day by day action plan. Even with all the information and guidance provided in this book, it's still not the same as waking up and having every single study hour laid out for you in a curated experience.

Having a carefully designed curriculum that takes you from

where you are right now to being ready for the bar exam, and which removes all questions and doubts about whether you are doing enough, doing the right things, or if you are on track for exam day, is incredibly valuable. Especially when it comes with the support of knowing that you're not doing it alone. Even the most disciplined among us can benefit from being held accountable, encouraged, and supported.

There's just something about working with someone who can lead you through something important in your life; something which has painful consequences if it goes wrong. That is why we have professionals like wedding planners, business coaches, bar exam tutors, and personal trainers. In fact, what may seem at first glance to be ironic, is that even the people who arguably need the least help of all of us: billion-dollar business owners, elite athletes, and professional entertainers, hire out help. Usually, they have *many* coaches to help them.

Why would a pro athlete being paid millions of dollars a year need a coach? Why would a Grammy-winning recording artist need a voice coach? Why would a CEO of a billion-dollar company need a productivity coach? Why would an Oscar-winning actor need coaching? Why would anyone who is the best in the world at what they do need or use a coach?

Perhaps they're the best in the world at what they do *because* they use a coach.

When results matter, and when you realize the high price you pay financially, mentally, emotionally, and with lost time that can never be recouped if you don't get results, working with a professional makes sense and is actually the *least expensive* decision you could make.

I talk to bar exam repeaters every single day. Every one of them -

if it were possible to turn back time - would happily trade the last six months, two years, or ten years of not being licensed for my coaching fee. Because on the balance, not being licensed has been a much steeper price to pay.

If you want to have a discussion about it, just reach out.

ABOUT THE AUTHOR

Jessica Klein is a former prosecutor turned bar exam coach. She decided to trade in the excitement of trial work and busy dockets for the opportunity to help others take their seat at counsel table. She self-studied and passed the California and Virginia bar exams after developing a revolutionary, simple, and effective study approach called The Klein Method.

   Now Jessica helps others take their rightful place at counsel table using her unorthodox method. Armed with an empowering and approachable style, nobody does bar prep like she does.

 facebook.com/fckthebar

 instagram.com/fckthebar

Made in the USA
Coppell, TX
31 May 2023

17559534R00095